Nyimpini Mabunda

TAKE CHARGE

Life lessons on the road to CEO

Jonathan Ball Publishers
JOHANNESBURG · CAPE TOWN · LONDON

All rights reserved.
No part of this publication may be reproduced or transmitted, in any form or by any means, without prior permission from the publisher or copyright holder.

© Text Nyimpini Cuthbert Mabunda 2022
© Published edition 2022 Jonathan Ball Publishers

Originally published in South Africa in 2022 by
JONATHAN BALL PUBLISHERS
A division of Media24 (Pty) Ltd
PO Box 33977
Jeppestown
2043

Reprinted in 2022(twice)

ISBN: 978-1-77619-200-7
eBook ISBN: 978-1-77619-201-4

Every effort has been made to trace the copyright holders and to obtain their permission for the use of copyright material. The publishers apologise for any errors or omissions and would be grateful to be notified of any corrections that should be incorporated in future editions of this book.

www.jonathanball.co.za
www.twitter.com/JonathanBallPub
www.facebook.com/JonathanBallPublishers

Cover by Sean Robertson
Cover photo by George Oosthuizen/Howling Hound Photography
Design and typesetting by Johan Koortzen
Set in Sabon MT Pro 11 on 16pt
Printed by CTP Printers, Cape Town

CONTENTS

About the author — v
Foreword by Reuel Khoza — vi
Reflections by Robbie Brozin — xi
Dedication & Acknowledgements — xiii
Preface — xvi

1. Born a warrior — 1
2. The deep end: 1992–1995 — 15
3. On the road: How I got lost and found my way back — 29
4. Sometimes you need to slow down to go faster — 45
5. A giant leap in Uganda — 65
6. The red revolution — 85
7. Taking a no-gap year — 100
8. A B2B adventure — 115
9. Grow yourself — 130
10. Grow others — 143
11. The importance of physical and mental well-being — 160
12. Leading through imperfection — 176
13. My personal board of directors — 190

ABOUT THE AUTHOR

Nyimpini Mabunda is the CEO of General Electric in southern Africa and chairman of U.S.–South Africa Business Council at the US Chamber of Commerce. A passionate devotee of innovation and digital transformation, he has built a proven track record of excellence over two decades in leadership positions across a variety of industries, including fast-moving consumer goods, telecommunications and financial services.

Mabunda attained his first degree at the University of Cape Town at age 18, began his professional career with one of the world's leading consumer goods companies at 19 and was promoted to line manager at just 21. He has brought an entrepreneurial mind-set to sales, marketing, strategy and general management for market-leading multinational organisations across Africa and Europe.

A regular speaker at events, as well as being a highly sought-after coach and mentor to some of the brightest young talent Africa has to offer, Mabunda sits on several boards as non-executive director and non-executive chairman.

FOREWORD
BY DR REUEL J KHOZA

German playwright, poet and philosopher Johann Christoph Friedrich von Schiller opines, 'He who has done his best for his own time has lived for all time'. Nyimpini Cuthbert Mabunda's quest for summitting the corporate apex epitomises this in fascinating fashion. His odyssey to date is characterised by momentous defining phases, bursting with lessons in adventure, entrepreneurship, management and business leadership.

Take Charge is an autobiography. It is, however, more than a biography. It is a generational slice of life, an abundant individual life immersed in interdependence. Nyimpini was ambitious, curious and observant as a youngster; inquisitive, analytical and diligent as a young adult both at university and in career life. Though serious, *Take Charge* is written as a narrative in the first person, in characteristic African storytelling manner. Captivating, at times verging on thrilling.

Bucking the orthodoxy that maintains that the ideal age to start schooling is seven, Nyimpini commenced at age five. Accompanying his school principal mother to school he slid into school like a duck takes to water. The family retail business enabled him to dabble in commercial transactions at an early age. These two factors of his formative years enabled him to enter secondary school aged 10, to finish his bachelor's degree and a postgraduate diploma at 19 and realise his first managerial position at 21.

The stage was set for a rich and enriching corporate business career. By now Nyimpini had clearly chosen to take charge, to determine his own destiny. To purposefully make things happen, with him firmly in the driver's seat. To actively and deliberately avoid the prevailing culture of entitlement somewhat characteristic of his era.

What is in a name? Quite a lot, depending on parental intent and the response of the individual named. Nyimpini means 'at war' or 'during a war'. Nyimpini was born to an enlightened African Shangaan family during the period of the 1976 student uprising. This was not without significance to Nyimpini's parents. They knew their son was going to face challenges that amount to a war: apartheid – politics of oppression and suppression; economics of exploitation and exclusion from the economic mainstream. Nyimpini himself was to come to the realisation that the world, particularly the corporate world, is competitive to a fault, a dog-eat-dog arena – that it is a jungle out there. Business leadership, Nyimpini was later to conclude, was about survival where you do not necessarily mourn the underperformance of a contestant.

Nyimpini's cardinal drive, his key objective, was to be a CEO and, having read *Take Charge*, I am convinced that his path to that position was inexorable. His motif force is that there is never a permanent blockage to your destination; you are at your best when you are you, so play to your strengths. Authenticity matters. Achieve, achieve, achieve! Authenticity and an abiding sense of destiny matter to Nyimpini. Each milestone in his corporate odyssey to date is a significant building block towards a clearly articulated destination.

His corporate journey from when he joined Procter & Gamble, through the various corporations and entrepreneurial detours, into running a cluster of Nando's franchises and a putative corporate sabbatical, to his current position as CEO of GE Southern Africa, has been purposeful, deliberate and determined – key considerations in corporate leadership success.

Significantly, Nyimpini enjoys challenging tasks, thrives on stretching himself and is motivated by achievement. He loves living under pressure, being under the spotlight and having ultimate accountability. His mantra is, why can't I do it despite my putative disadvantaged background? He is convinced that he can always bring something of substantive value to the table. These are signal pieces of advice to would-be business leaders.

Ambitious, aspirant young executives are given to incessant pursuit of their careers, pausing only when they break for that cherished executive development programme at a reputable business school. Nyimpini understood this and appreciated more. He treasured the revitalising role of a sabbatical in executive career development. A time to reflect, for personal renewal, lasting about a year. He fully understood the Sotho idiomatic expression: *Go tshetshela morago a se go tshaba*. Slowing down or even retreating is not flight. It is a way of gathering momentum.

Nyimpini strongly believes in self-development. He clearly heeded Plato's admonition that 'the first and best victory is to conquer self'. Taking charge behove him to do this. Internal locus of control was fundamental to his life orientation – through various postings in different geographies, working for different companies; through taking advantage of accessible executive development programmes; and, very importantly, through strategically gathering wisdom from senior colleagues, Nyimpini gained unassailable self-mastery.

Manifest practical elements of his sustainable self-mastery include keeping the company of colleagues who continually challenge you; regularly sharpening the saw, realising that while what brought you here is essential to give you historical perspective, but it is not sufficient to take you there – the future is not what it used to be. Nyimpini subscribes to the notion that to keep leading you must keep learning. Appreciation of culture, be it generic or corporate, underscores all these.

In Nyimpini's world view, effective responsive leadership must perforce be both passionate and compassionate. Passion focuses on self-development and compassion on developing others. Regarding the latter, it behoves a conscientious and responsive leader to identify potential superstars and to purposefully develop them. One needs to realise that talented people are not a threat to oneself but could even add lustre to one's growing business leadership. Growing others frees you up to explore and innovate. Together in synergy you lift the organisation to loftier heights. When you grow others, you increase and improve capacity to deliver. Lift as you rise.

Nyimpini also believes in assembling a 'personal board of directors'. This proposes that you surround yourself with sapient corporate elders who are bold enough to provide you with critical feedback, addressing your vulnerabilities. Beware of uncritical praise singers. Occasional vituperative comment from seniors who care about your development will not necessarily harm. Look for areas where you may be vulnerable and heed germane admonition. Consider Elon Musk's advice that you may not necessarily agree with some, but learn from them anyway.

Lately, governance and leadership have loomed large in Nyimpini's corporate life. Big governance fiascos intrigue him. These include corruption scandals surrounding such major corporations as Bain and ABB, as well as the leading international audit firms. There are crucial fundamental lessons to be learnt from these ignominious corporate failures.

Throughout his rather active and rewarding career, Nyimpini has deciphered some lessons and success pointers. Among these are that nothing is really impossible, we just do not know how to tackle those apparent impossibilities today. We have boundless capability. Ours is to be breakthrough-intensive. Quite often, we believe we are engaging in thinking – when in reality we are not, we tend to be on 'autopilot'. We can often surprise ourselves if we care to think. For successful executive work, we need to take the trouble to comprehend how things work.

In dealing with today's increasingly complex situations, we need to engage in continual learning, constantly reinventing ourselves – we are essentially work in progress. Improvement is infinite, one can always get better. Of crucial importance, beyond the bottom line there is the horizon: we must focus on saving and enhancing the natural environment. The interplay amongst people, profit and planet is of paramount importance. Having travelled to more than forty countries before the age of forty, Nyimpini is convinced that curiosity is fuel for greater achievement.

Whither Nyimpini? He fakes ignorance about this but of one thing he is sure: the future bristles with opportunities. He would inter alia wish to have broader impact through board directorship, executive coaching, guest lecturing at business schools and creating jobs through entrepreneurship.

In conclusion, I exhort you to read Nyimpini's account of a decisive, diligent and dedicated approach to business. It is written in captivating autobiographical style in a bid to hold a mirror to up-and-coming executives. You might just spare yourself the gruelling business school life but learn just as much by reading *Take Charge*. It is as informative as it is inspiring. No dull moment through the pages. I commend *Take Charge* as a must-read.

REFLECTIONS
BY ROBBIE BROZIN

South Africa is a remarkable, miraculous country. For me, there have been two pillars of deep inspiration. The first is a blessing from the Lubavitcher Rebbe, Rabbi Menachem Schneerson, that South Africa will be good until the Messiah comes and, after that, even better!

And the second is that we have been blessed with one of the best constitutions in the world. The preamble to the Constitution is a beautifully constructed, simple but immensely powerful vision for our country. It is a vision that, I believe, has the power to 'build a united and democratic South Africa able to take its rightful place as a sovereign state in the family of nations', as the document says.

However, any document, any vision or building, is just an empty promise. It takes people and, more importantly, people of integrity, humility and action to realise potential and ideals.

Nyimpini's story, from his humble upbringing in Rolle through to his experiences in some of the most inspirational corporates in the world and culminating in his maturity as a seasoned executive board member, mentor, husband and father, gives me the confidence that South Africa has the people to deliver on this ideal.

Nyimpini's curiosity and approach to leadership – through servant leadership and the ability to believe in yourself, even when doubts claw at your subconscious – are practical lessons and inspirations that are relevant to every reader who believes that the preamble to the Constitution is a real reminder of how the struggle has been won – but that, for us to reach for the best in the country, we need to reach for the best in ourselves. His often-tough choices have mirrored the vision and the ideals of the preamble, something that he can be so proud of.

His best choice of the lot was to marry Mosima, and she has been an incredible support and stable influence, really underpinning the thought that it is easier to face the future without fear if we do not do so alone. Mosima, I salute you!

Rabbi Lord Jonathan Sacks describes a leader and a 'mensch' as a 'person whose greatness is lightly worn, who cares about the people others often ignore, the fatherless, the widow, and the stranger, who spends as much time with the people at the margins of society as with the elites, who is courteous to everyone equally and who receives respect because he gives respect'. Nyimpini encompasses this description perfectly.

Nyimpini's time at Nando's was far too short for us. I was personally deeply regretful of his decision to rejoin Diageo but totally understood and respected it. To have been a small but positive part of his remarkable career is such a privilege; I take immense joy in writing this piece, and am honoured to do so. I know that his father is beaming down with such pride at how Nyimpini has honoured him and his family name.

DEDICATION & ACKNOWLEDGEMENTS

I dedicate this book to my late father, Mcovelo Leonard Mabunda. I still marvel at his sheer brilliance, resourcefulness, supreme intellect, talent in communication – especially his legendary public speaking – problem-solving skills and, above all, being a loving husband and a father to me and my siblings. I am what I am today because of his selfless coaching and mentorship, and his role modelling through exemplary behaviour.

Two of his favourite maxims, which still drive me today, were 'Aim higher, my son' and 'Nothing will make me happier than my family staying united and supportive of one another long after I am gone'. I sincerely hope we continue to make you proud, Dad!

This book would not have been possible were it not for the encouragement and support of my incredible wife Mosima who, in addition to reviewing seemingly countless pages, pushed me to keep writing, even on days when I was not feeling inspired. She believed in this project with infectious passion. Thank you, love – this is the product of us at our best.

My children are such an inspiration! I thank them for allowing me the space to write this book. Though they were supportive, I must nonetheless apologise to them for being distracted during the writing phase. I hope that, upon reading this book, they will appreciate why Dad had to make the sacrifice. More importantly, now that the book is finished, we will catch up. I have missed our time together. Here's to Amu, Nyiko and Tšhegofatšo.

I would also like to thank my mother – my first educator, formally as my teacher at school, but then in lessons that continued into late hours at home and throughout my life. I have never encountered a more loving, loyal, caring and hard-working individual. That work ethic no doubt drove me to my career heights.

My siblings – Mashangu, Tingana, Mugiyo, Hlulekile and Khensani – you are my pillars of strength. We have been through so much together. Thank you for the fighting spirit.

Further recognition and thanks go to my teachers from primary school to university, all the line managers I worked with, coaches, mentors, my spiritual leaders, pastors and the teams with whom we delivered magic. Though I am celebrating my achievements and growth in this book, I am acutely aware that it was made possible only because of your selfless contributions to my life. I cannot mention you all by name, but most of you are mentioned in various sections of the book. From the bottom of my heart, thank you. It's true that it takes a village to raise a child and I was raised by all of you!

Which relatively unknown business executive is able to entice two South African business legends to generously contribute to his book? I don't know what I did to deserve it, but I am immensely grateful to Robbie Brozin, the legendary co-founder of Nando's – who just happens to be one of the world's most humble philanthropists – and Dr Reuel Khoza for their kind words and guidance on this project.

I have been led in my journey by watching Dr Khoza's leadership and governance work – particularly his high ethical standards. I am honoured.

I would like to thank Mteto Nyati, whose contributions initiated and closed this project. We met with Mteto to learn from his experience in publishing his own book, *Betting on a Darkie*, before getting started. I was so inspired and confident after our engagement that I decided to go ahead and complete the book before approaching a publisher.

On that note, I must thank the core team representing Jonathan Ball Publishers – Gill Moodie, Angela Voges and Caren van Houwelingen – for their expert assistance that has made the production process seamless and painless.

I am also indebted to Simbarashe Sialumba, Refilwe Tshabalala and Khensani Mthombeni for their roles as 'first readers' and providing helpful feedback to guide revisions of the manuscript. Aside from also taking time to review the manuscript, Shanthini Naidoo was originally responsible for putting me in touch with both my writer and my publisher, for which I am eternally grateful. Shanthini was generous in sharing her learnings from the publication of her own highly successful book, *Women in Solitary*.

Lastly, there are two special individuals who were most instrumental in this project: Brendan Peacock, my highly talented, creative and very patient writer and editor, and Lucy Balimba, the founder and managing director of Entelo Strategic Communications. Thank you for your help and guidance in bringing this project to fruition.

Inkomu!

PREFACE

How did you get to be a line manager at 21?
How did you position yourself to be a CEO candidate when it's so competitive out there?
How did you navigate corporate politics to get where you are?
Who did you have to network with?
How did you get an international assignment as a South African?
Who supported your career journey and how did you get them to do it?
I hear one needs a sponsor. How do you get one?
Should I do an MBA to enhance my growth?
Is it good to stay with one company for long, or am I better off changing employers to move up the ladder more quickly?
What's the role of a coach, and should I get one to move ahead in the corporate world?

These are some of the questions I have fielded most often as a business leader, and they come from all quarters: direct reports, mentees, coachees, friends, social media posts and journalists. I have been asked these questions, or their variants, so often that I decided the best way to make my career learnings accessible to anyone with an interest in curating their career would be to write this book.

The implementation of lockdown restrictions in South Africa in the second quarter of 2020 presented me with an opportunity to use what would have been my social time – which would typically have been spent travelling, attending conferences and dinners, playing golf and building relationships – to reflect on my career.

In sitting down to structure my thoughts and write, I realised just how significant this component of career growth can be, already beginning to answer some of the questions above. By eliminating commuting time and social engagements, I found hours with which to be productive in codifying my growth tactics and strategies to help others reach heights they perhaps thought unattainable.

I have been truly blessed in my life and career, growing up in a business-oriented family, becoming a student leader at the University of Cape Town at the age of 16, starting my professional career with a multinational at 19 and becoming a line manager at 21.

At 22 I ran a cash van operation and was responsible for direct employment of 50 people in a convenience and wholesale channel. At 28 I was a joint venture partner for Nando's, running 6 outlets I owned with a partner.

I spent years of my working life abroad in the UK and then Uganda, where I was appointed to my first CEO role at the age of 37. I went on to be a group executive at several multinationals, including Boston Consulting Group, Vodafone/Vodacom and GE.

At my current age, 45, I hold several high-impact external board roles in various sectors and sit on the boards of international organisations like the Young President's Organization (YPO) and the U.S.–South Africa Business Council (a division of the US Chamber of Commerce), where I serve as chairman.

There is much more I would still like to achieve, as much as I have led what I am told is an extraordinary life. I believe that the learnings, failings and work ethic that have together underpinned my career arc can be synthesised into the lessons for others in this book.

My family was not wealthy and I attended a public school in a homeland in pre-democratic South Africa. I was not an A-student and did not study accounting, engineering or science, nor did I study business as my primary degree. My university qualification was in social science and I began working in the marketing and sales stream.

I was neither overly popular nor a prefect, and I never played sport seriously or to any notable achievement. In that respect, my journey to a CEO was both atypical and profoundly 'normal' in that I worked hard, leveraged my strengths and consciously set out to achieve goals that would bring me ever closer to a leadership position.

I believe there are many potential senior leaders out there who simply lack the self-belief and toolkit to begin their own journey to the top. There are, as they say, many ways to skin a cat, and the world faces unprecedented disruption. If there was ever a time for someone to bring fresh ideas and a unique approach to leadership, that time is now.

I hope that this book will provide the inspired action necessary to develop new leaders who do not conform to the heavily criticised archetype of leaders of the past.

My intention behind writing this book was to inspire others to take charge of their career destiny, progress and journey. It's easy to think your work will 'speak' for itself, to focus on education or training and hope your achievements will drive your growth. The assumption that it will be possible to ride the wave of relevant policies like empowerment of women, diversity and inclusion or Broad-Based Black Economic Empowerment (BBBEE) – if you are in the designated groups – is also seductive. However, my contention is that 'God helps those who help themselves'.

One needs to be proactive and have a plan to stay ahead of the curve, and that plan needs to be grounded in insight and driven with focus. In this respect, a career is much like a marriage or a business: own it, drive it, make things happen and leave nothing to chance.

I am fortunate and privileged to have enjoyed a great business career outside of the corporate sphere, including successfully running my own businesses and working for one of the world's largest consulting firms.

I have leveraged the skills and insight gained from both of these undertakings, as well as my years as an executive coach, to share expertise with executives from non-competing companies and would now like to share my experience with you in the hope that it can help propel you along your career path.

I thoroughly enjoyed writing this book and learnt a great deal about myself in the process. I certainly hope you enjoy reading it.

I
BORN A WARRIOR

I was born in a tiny village called Rolle, in Mpumalanga, in 1976 – a year famous for the June 16 Soweto Uprising, which saw thousands of black schoolchildren lead a protest against the introduction of Afrikaans as a medium of instruction in the townships. My parents named me Nyimpini, which translates to 'at war' or 'a warrior', and I believe this was in many ways apposite for what was to come in my life.

My father later told me that since I was born just five months after the events of 16 June, it was clear that the country itself was at war and we all had to stand up and fight. As such, my given name was to remind him and people around us about the call to action.

I love our African culture because there's a meaning and a rich story to each of our names. We ought to take the hint from our parents' intentions, for they wished for something through each of us. It is no surprise that people born around that time carried names like Freedom, Matimba (power), Zamani (keep trying), Justice and Mayihlome (take up arms and fight), which spoke to the desire to topple the apartheid government.

I became a real fighter. I knew nothing would come easy in life, especially if you were among the most disadvantaged. Even among black people there were degrees of being disadvantaged: there were the Township Blacks living in Soweto and other former Transvaal townships, who were – as a rule – better off than most because they were more than likely working and literate.

Then there were people like me, far away from urban areas, living in Bantustans – or homelands, as they were better known – with no viable, sustainable local economy. People there relied on government grants and those formally employed held a very limited number of public sector jobs, such as police officers or teachers.

The education delivered in these areas was inferior, through under-resourced schools and teachers who were barely qualified – if they were qualified at all. Back then you didn't need a matric pass to become a teacher – all that was required to attend training as a teacher was to pass Standard 8, or Grade 10 in today's terminology.

That is the kind of school I attended until I completed Standard 5 (Grade 7) – Daniye Primary School. It was a public school with next to nothing by way of facilities. I vividly remember studying under a marula tree, with a makeshift chalkboard propped up on my thighs.

Looking back at growing up in Rolle, with no running water or electricity, and studying at Daniye, with no actual classrooms, under teachers who were trying their best, I think the lesson I was really learning was that allowing an underprivileged upbringing to affect our confidence in our ability to compete is a mistake.

Kenyan athletes without fancy sports shoes, professional trainers or advanced facilities frequently beat the rest of the world's runners. From this it is important to learn that, as difficult as our circumstances may be, we cannot use that to justify lagging.

Today, my children are very privileged, able to attend some of the finest private schools in South Africa. Again, to illustrate the point, there is a school in the Vembe district of Limpopo – a public school with very basic facilities and no school fees – which is consistently one of the top schools in the country, based on matric results.

I believe nobody should be intimidated by external factors or apparent limitations. We should give ourselves permission to compete despite an unequal footing.

That said, I was not at the bottom of the pyramid. The truth is, I grew up relatively privileged in the context of the Bantustan. I was born to a mother who was a schoolteacher, earning a monthly income from the government. My father was also employed by the government as a health inspector, so he too was bringing home a monthly income.

Living in a household with educated parents who were not caught up in the migrant labour system afforded me a relatively normal life and the benefit of parental guidance. My privilege went beyond being a middle-class family in a homeland under apartheid – my parents decided to start a business. From 1978 they ran a retail outlet selling groceries and fast foods, and by 1988 the business had grown to include a hardware shop, a clothing shop and a butchery. Business was good and we were living well. The first 10 years of my life were incredibly inspirational as our family thrived along with the business.

I was comfortable, but I worked hard on a variety of fronts from a very young age. I worked as a shop assistant from when I was old enough, which is in keeping with the entrepreneurial tendency to maintain family oversight of the business. We siblings were allocated roles, like working the tills, as a form of financial control.

If we weren't old enough to handle the till points, we'd be picking and replenishing stock at the counter service to ensure that daily stock counts balanced. By the age of 12 I was driving a Toyota Stout 4x4 to deliver building materials like cement, doors and window frames to customers. I didn't have a licence, but that didn't matter to anyone.

My dad had grown his work portfolio and became a homeland politician, elected as a member of Parliament for our region. He was also made speaker of the Cabinet, and in that role grew close to the Chief Minister of Gazankulu, Professor Hudson Ntsanwisi. The chief minister would come and visit our home in Rolle and spend hours with us, so we grew up knowing him as a family friend. I was inspired by this highly educated, charismatic leader, who was also accessible.

I was motivated by my father's practical and sensible use of his savings to start a business, expand it and then become a community leader. He worked hard and involved us in the business from the beginning, though he never allowed that to be a reason for our slipping up with our schoolwork. We should succeed in both our schoolwork and involvement in the business, he said, which taught me that we always have more capacity than we give ourselves credit for.

We can do a lot more with the time we have if we are disciplined and make a few sacrifices along the way – especially those things that may derail us from our intended course. From a young age I was learning to be involved in multiple enterprises at once, and to persist in juggling them through hard work.

So, I grew up in business and I believe it is in my blood. So is winning. But that had to start somewhere.

I was naturally inclined to love learning. As the son of a teacher, my mother's passion for education was infectious. She had the patience for the vocation and her great talent was to build others – including me and my siblings.

She too worked hard, first completing every workday as a teacher and then going to help run the business after hours. I tended to be by her side, wherever she went. The apron strings were strong because I would accompany my mother to school from the age of two, sitting in her office and playing while she taught. I refused to be left at home, crying until she relented.

This went on until I turned four, when one of the teachers decided to take me into her class with other kids who were years older. I began participating in the schoolwork and enjoyed myself, doing well enough to pass the assessments comfortably. I was kept in the class and that's how I ended up matriculating at the age of 15, starting university before my 16th birthday.

As much as I advocate for hard work, there is a lot to be said for chance and using the opportunities that present themselves – seizing the moment. There are times in our lives when things just happen. They come our way unexpectedly and we must learn to take advantage of them.

When I once asked a CEO how he had made it to the top of the ladder, seeking advice about how I could do the same, he told me that, aside from financial acumen, there were five qualities he believed an individual needed to possess to be a business leader: a strategic mind, a high-functioning intellect, emotional intelligence, great stakeholder management and the ability to mobilise support. Still, these would not guarantee passage to the C-suite, he said, because the essential ingredient is *luck*. He reminded me that many people have talent and potential, but with so few CEO roles available, only one out of thousands of employees within a large organisation can be CEO at any one time, for example. Some luck is necessary.

This happened at Old Mutual in 2020, as the candidate who was not preferred initially was in line when the newly appointed CEO fell out with the board barely 18 months into the job. When the board asked the COO to step in while they searched for a successor, he did such a good job at stabilising the business and delivering results that there was no reason not to elevate him to the CEO role permanently.

Positioning is a crucial skill in building a career and it is the prerequisite for luck. Find yourself, by design, in the right places so that when things happen, they come your way. Then grasp the opportunity.

I have watched many a black leader be too humble to take advantage of the situation facing them. Fears of being viewed as the beneficiary of nepotism or employment equity policy can be particularly troublesome, even as the children of successful leaders – who have been mentored by their parents to become skilled leaders themselves – of other races are moving through the ranks.

All parents do what they can. They leverage networks, make phone calls, open doors. Leverage what you have, and don't worry so much about perception.

It was my good fortune that my mother was an educator and that, through boredom, I began attending school early, accelerating my development and education. My good fortune extended to the family business, where my interest did not end at the family retail stores. When I was six I was my mother's trusted salesman of 'ice blocks', a flavoured powdered cordial or liquid concentrate we made into a beverage, poured into plastic bags and froze overnight.

The production process took place every evening and in the morning we'd pack a cooler bag into my mom's bakkie so we could sell the ice blocks at school. The hot weather combined with competitive pricing and my burgeoning sales skills made them a hit.

I was thus given lessons in hard work by both my parents. My mother taught me multitasking and the reward for delivering results. We were always incentivised: if I sold everything in the cooler box, I would get a chocolate. When corporates today talk of long-term and short-term incentives in remuneration packages, this resonates well with me!

My business acumen was honed by the responsibilities my dad gave me from a very young age. He insisted on treating customers with respect – something which many may have thought unnecessary since our business was the first of its kind in the area and therefore practically a monopoly. We may have had a captive market, but my dad always emphasised that other businesses could obtain licences and open nearby, so we needed to make sure our customers supported us. On reflection, the service levels and innovations like stock assortment, combo deals and credit extension set us apart.

I learnt to give back to the community too, since both my parents were charitable to the community around us. There were countless trips using my dad's truck to take kids to local soccer games, fully sponsored by my family. We bought the team kits and supported tournaments.

My parents fixed local government schools, built sports facilities, donated books and so on. As a child I would sometimes be angry at my mother for giving away things we were supposed to sell. I was fixated on the profit, feeling that strangers were taking advantage of her. Yet our business continued to grow from strength to strength as word got out that we were helping the community. In turn, the community continued to buy from us. Years later, this would inform my approach to corporate social investment.

I sometimes wonder how transferable these experiences are, especially to someone whose background did not involve a family business, but I believe the relevance stems from the similarity of circumstances in my generation. Many black South Africans of my generation and older grew up in an informal business of some sort, like street vending, knitting jerseys and blankets, running a spaza shop or owning a taxi in a township.

Everyone knows an aunt or an uncle who runs an informal business. My mother was brought up by my grandmother because my grandfather was a migrant labourer who came home only a few times a year. He provided for his family and deeply loved his seven kids, of whom my mother was the first born.

My grandfather was not well paid, so my grandmother sold whatever she could to supplement the family income. I remember that, long after several of her children were independent, her speciality was buying things like salt, tobacco, ground nuts and maize in bulk 50 kg bags and then repackaging the goods into smaller, affordable sizes for resale. Most people were hustling daily themselves, and could therefore only buy enough maize or other items for that day's use.

Years later I was appointed Head of Channel at Procter & Gamble, to run a wholesale and informal distribution business where we needed to repack items for spaza shop distribution. Lessons I learnt as a youngster are still so applicable.

My mother learnt a great deal about business from informal retail run by her mother, and although my father was the face of the business and it became synonymous with him, it's common knowledge that it was my mom's idea to start the business, which is still running back in Rolle. Even while she was still employed as a teacher, she was selling goods from home and was successful, inspired by her upbringing and planting the seed of the family business that was to come.

I believe we all have stories like this in our backgrounds from which we can draw inspiration. Growing up under apartheid and even into democracy post-1994, there was so much hardship for black people in South Africa that our parents had to overcome many obstacles for us to be where we are today.

Being appointed as the leader of a business can often require resuscitating the business from setbacks or overcoming challenges the previous incumbent could not cope with. Given our backgrounds, I believe as black people we have a lot to draw on to help us succeed against the odds. Think of the taxi fleet owners who started with one taxi and today have many vehicles, when obtaining finance in an informal and unregulated industry was practically impossible.

Richard Maponya, who built businesses in Soweto, still needed access to certain wholesalers to pick up stock. These were people whose shops were rebuilt following riots and protests, and which survived many hardships in an environment that was not only competitive but subject to more difficult trading conditions than the businesses of our white counterparts. We can put this experience to use in our business careers.

I learnt an important lesson in 1985 while I was in primary school, when the school principal at Daniye Primary – in an effort to raise the bar of academic excellence – announced to all pupils in Standard 3 (the equivalent of Grade 5, my grade at the time) that, as long as they achieved a minimum average of 90 per cent, the top three pupils would be allowed to skip Standard 4 and progress to Standard 5.

This brought on a lot of excitement and tension in class. The tension came from the competitive spirit – there were more than 80 kids in the grade who wanted to be in the top three, and we worked our backsides off that year.

My mother would wake me very early in the morning to study before I washed and got ready for school. I was given time off from selling at the shop after school to go study. I didn't even go with my father to buy stock, which was my favourite thing to do. Every spare moment I had was given over to studying.

That year, the average mark for the entire grade went up by 20 per cent, and I came third. What a delight! This was the power of using your desire to achieve something, and what a pleasure it was to be celebrated by those around me. To this day, I will go the extra mile because of the power of recognition, the pleasure of achieving the reward.

I understood from a very young age the concept of incentive, which is probably how I landed up in sales. The gratification of earning a commission was exciting to me, as was knowing that if you didn't bring in the numbers you got much less pay. This has given me an appreciation that nothing in life is guaranteed.

Hard work pays – no effort, no reward. Nothing for mahala. There I was, in January 1986, a Standard 5 pupil. The three of us had to prove our worth because our new classmates were envious of us, knowing we had skipped a grade. Even some of the teachers were not supportive of the principal's move, thinking they would have to put in extra work to help us catch up with the rest of the cohort.

The end-of-year examinations were externally set and assessed, and ultimately it was up to us to pass well so that there could be no accusations of unfair play or favouritism. I managed to pass well and was promoted to Standard 6, the first grade of high school. It became clear to me then that not everything in life needed to be linear. The schooling system and its grades were set to meet the normal distribution curve and lowest common denominator – the middle 80 per cent. I was determined from then onwards that I would not be defined by this bell curve.

Although I was strong academically, my parents encouraged me to participate in leisure and sporting activities too, so in 1985 they bought me a BMX, which I named Striker. I became a changed man. I participated in competitions for our area and became champion of my village. I competed with kids from other areas and won a silver medal.

Just like with academics, when I came home with a B grade or a silver medal for cycling, my dad – being a perfectionist and ultra-competitive – would want to know more about the person who got an A or won the race. Who was he or she? Where did they live? By how much and in what areas did they better me? What did I intend to do about it?

Though there was pressure to be the best, these discussions were pragmatic and pointed to areas where I could leverage either a privilege or an advantage. As an example, my dad would ask if I was spending enough time doing homework with my mother's help. We were one of the few families who, by this stage, had a generator to provide electricity, meaning I could study at almost any time, while other kids struggled to do so.

We all have certain advantages, and we need to find them. It's often too easy to see the things working against us, while not making enough use of our own unique blessings. Using these to become better through leveraging our advantage can help us find our unique proposition. No two backgrounds are identical, and it is more powerful to build on your strengths than to pity your weaknesses in achieving greatness.

The combination of starting school at four and skipping a grade meant that by January 1987 I started high school at the age of ten. True to form, given my parents' bold standards, I was sent 250 km away to a boarding school in Giyani, in what is now the Limpopo province.

This was the beginning of my five-year high school journey at Kheto High School. This school was special – the ultimate education experience in the homeland. The chief minister's children and grandchildren, and other parliamentarians' kids, joined the progeny of the wealthy and the highest achievers from Gazankulu at this school.

Kheto was Gazankulu's centre of academic excellence. We were in the company of greatness, inspired by the excellence of our peers. Being among the best and competing with them became intensely important to me. I was once told by somebody that in a race of one you always win. Don't isolate yourself – you must benchmark, otherwise you will be lying to yourself.

Being at the school was humbling. Nearly every kid there was used to being number one in their class. I found myself a middling student by Kheto standards, though the teachers found my tender age fascinating. One teacher, Mr Nkuna, called me Ten Years right up to the day I matriculated. I didn't let that label get to me, and throughout my life, where I have often been the youngest in every situation, I have been determined not to be patronised or underestimated.

Boarding school at the age of ten was an eye-opener. I needed to grow up very quickly, and I was barely mature enough to handle it. I had to show that I qualified to sit at the same table as everyone else.

This kind of confidence to punch above my weight is the attitude I have adopted throughout my life, whenever I have been in situations where there have been competitors with more experience or who were more capable. My ability to progress, survive and even excel in high school without my parents instructing or guiding me built a lot of confidence.

As with many things in life, the acceleration in some spheres left me disadvantaged in others – particularly on the sports field. I had a height and weight disadvantage for sports and, as a result, ended up not continuing with the many sports I had played at primary school.

Another negative of growing up in a prominent family in business, education and politics was that I ran the risk of being spoiled, and to some extent I was. It meant people often did things to try to impress my parents. For example, my mother had become principal of the primary school I attended, and this meant teachers were often helpful to me to get on her good side.

As a family business, we also employed many people and supported other families. There were therefore many in our community who would serve us, especially given that my father was a relatively powerful homeland politician who also sat on a tender board. We were well taken care of, through efforts to impress my father.

Boarding school was an equaliser. The other pupils were also from relatively privileged families and, generally speaking, I did not stand out. For the first time, nobody knew me – I was an ordinary pupil and I had to do things for myself, like doing my laundry and making meals after the dining hall's 6 p.m. dinner if we were still hungry. There was an element of survival about it all.

High school also came with lessons in financial management. Initially, my father had worried about my ability to manage the pocket money I was given, and back in those days most kids did not use banking services. Allowances for groceries and snacks to supplement hostel food were given in cash.

Every Thursday we were allowed out for two hours of shopping. My dad thought I was not mature enough to make my allowance last through the whole month, so he found a matric pupil who was instructed to keep my money and provide me with a stipend of R2 per day.

He was the gatekeeper and, as trust in this arrangement grew, Justice Mafuwane saw that I was disciplined and started giving me money for two or three days at a time, and then whole weeks. Ultimately, he would come to hand over my R60 for the whole month.

This money management training taught me a lot about taking a risk on people and I also learnt to let go of total control. I learnt that we have a responsibility to protect and reward those who honour us with trust, instead of embarrassing them through poor personal conduct. My trust in employees has almost always been rewarded instead of abused.

There is a point in all our lives where we stand on our own and take responsibility. This is an opportunity to gain confidence when presented with a challenge. Too often, however, we can be afraid to take career risks or do something we don't feel ready for.

Think of a time when you needed to act in your boss's position and realised it was not as complex as you thought. At what point do we call ourselves ready? In whose eyes do we need to be ready? We all know someone who has been denied a promotion by their employer because they were said to not be ready, and in disappointment they left and accepted a senior role from a competing company where they did a brilliant job.

At times we take the opinion of those we respect or are senior to us as definitive of our abilities. One of the best pieces of advice I was ever given is that you know yourself best, so you are in the best position to make judgements about your capabilities.

Possibly the most daunting challenge of my high school career came at the end of 1988, my second year at Kheto. Our family driver arrived at the school unexpectedly and told us that my parents felt my sister Tingana – my elder by two years – and I needed to come home for a weekend visit. The driver was very cagey about the reason, but insisted we accompany him.

Even before our arrival at our family home we were shocked to see that the family business had been burnt down. It was the first time the business had ever closed. We were naturally confused but knew something was terribly wrong and found my mother inside our house wearing a grim expression, surrounded by her siblings and my gran.

I asked to see my younger sister and was taken to some elders who broke the devastating news that eight-year-old Hlulekile had been locked up with two employees, Mama Gift and Sisi Eunice, by thugs who had poured petrol over them and set them alight. Eunice had managed to escape and survived with burns, but Gift and Hlulekile had not.

This cruel act had been directed at my father, whom the thugs were sent to kill on the eve of elections as the result of political rivalry. Failing to find him, they thought they could hit him hardest by killing his last-born child.

Hit us hard they did. I remember that day like it was yesterday, and I still wonder what kind of woman Hluli would have grown up to be. We know the truth behind the murders because the thugs were arrested and served time for what they did. Some turned state witness and entered a plea bargain for confessing.

The pain of losing Hluli in such a brutal way – with our family not even being able to see the bodies because both were burnt beyond recognition – still hurts me today when I think about it. Such anger and violence against children remain shocking to me.

After the weekend visit, during which we buried Hluli, my sister and I went back to school in time to sit for exams. My dad insisted we go through with writing them to avoid repeating the year, but it was an instruction with a dual purpose – he didn't want us to crumble in sorrow and give our enemies any satisfaction. He taught us that when we suffer setbacks, miss goals or are struck down, we need to bounce back even stronger and make up for the setback.

Surprises will happen along our journeys. Sad events, bad news and even sorrow await us, but resilience is demonstrated in how we respond. In our professional lives, recruiters will look for problem-solving skills and an ability to grow and cope with change. If we have experienced challenges and setbacks in other spheres of our lives, what lessons have we learnt? Ultimately, all lessons count in the university of life.

By stark contrast, the highlight of attending boarding school for me was in 1990, when Nelson Mandela was released from prison. At the age of 13, I tried to understand and contextualise the significance of his release, even though at that age I was not politically inclined. While I knew Mandela had been in prison for many years, as the child of a homeland politician we were not really encouraged to discuss such things, since in many ways the homeland government system was seen as an extension of the separatist control system of the apartheid government.

I was surprised when, on 2 February 1990, ahead of Mandela's release, the school principal, Mr Siska, opened the hostel gates and allowed pupils and teachers to march into town to celebrate. There were a lot of people singing and enjoying what was a watershed moment in South

Africa's history. I was shocked to see another side of our otherwise very quiet and strait-laced principal.

Some of our teachers led political lives outside of school to an extent we could not have guessed, like Mr Mhlongo, who went on to become a mayor in the ANC government. There is something to be said for patience and waiting for your turn to come, never losing sight of your objectives. Our struggle-hero teachers, many of whom we thought had supported the homeland system, suddenly became unleashed and took a stand.

This irritated the leaders of Gazankulu greatly – especially the chief minister, who had his own political party, the Ximoko Party. He immediately ordered the closure of the school hostels because he felt this was where politically inclined individuals were plotting and gathering support for overthrowing the homeland system.

Many of us, whose family homes were far from the school, became homeless overnight. We needed to make a plan quickly. My sister and I were just about to start our matric year so it was inconvenient to move to another school. Our parents decided we should stay in Giyani and find lodging for our final year.

They asked relatives in Giyani if we could stay with them, though this was tough for us. Despite coping with boarding school for years, it was an unfamiliar environment – and even though we were related, we had not spent much time together before.

The house was large enough to accommodate everyone, but we were arriving to bedrooms that were already shared, creating an extra challenge of finding space to study. We also had to commute for half an hour each way, and now found ourselves back under 'parental' control for the first time in years. This was even more intense than having a boarding master.

Regardless of the changes in our living arrangements, 1991 was a great year and I learnt to become agile. I realised that as human beings we are adaptable and should not be daunted by changes in our circumstances. We need to work with whatever confronts us.

2
THE DEEP END: 1992–1995

I began studying at the University of Cape Town in 1992. Although this was 1 860 km from home, I had been told by my aunt – who had attended UCT – that my choice of tertiary institution mattered in terms of my employability and my CV. She was also adamant I should study what I loved and had a passion for, because it would be easier to do well.

My aunt had taken the opportunity to study at UCT when apartheid began to crumble, and she had loved her time there. She completed a master's degree in 1991, the year before I started there, and was amazed by the step up from homeland universities such as the University of Venda and of Transkei. Believing I was academically gifted, she encouraged me to follow in her footsteps.

Though UCT and Wits University were both known to be strong institutions, I was typically single-minded in deciding to follow in my aunt's footsteps, applying only to UCT. To reduce the risk, however, I applied for three degrees – accounting, business science in marketing and, as a backup, a social science degree. I decided all I had to do was get accepted and then decide what I wanted to do once I was there.

My father loved higher learning of all kinds and was something of an unfulfilled intellectual in the lines of work he pursued. He was close to my aunt, who lectured at a teacher training college, but he was also quick to associate with anyone who was well educated. He had saved money for his kids to attend university and his preference was for us to follow other callings to diversify our family's skills, but in this respect he was to get a surprise.

I broke the news to my dad that I wasn't going into a scientific field and, although he was disappointed, he wasn't one to override my desires. As it turns out, I didn't get enough points to get into accounting or business science, but was accepted into social science. I compared the curriculum of the degree I really wanted – business science – with my options in the social science stream in order to choose the courses that would most closely match, so I could leave university with virtually the same knowledge.

Social science was a three-year degree, as opposed to the four-year term of business science, but at that time students from the homelands were required first to complete an academic support programme (ASP), because our education was considered inferior even to township schools in urban areas.

The support programme was intended to bridge the gap between our Bantustan matric and what our peers were considered to have, converting a three-year degree into four years to ease us in. This was the pet hate of every black student who went to white-dominated institutions, generally, but there was a stipulation in place that if you excelled in the ASP you could join the main class within the first year.

I hate wasting time, so I worked hard and completed the degree in three years. However, this left me short of a business science equivalent, so I stayed on for another year to study a postgraduate diploma in marketing management, which was the kind of specialised course I was seeking. In content, I had now studied two qualifications that were very closely aligned with the degree I wanted originally.

This may seem like a risky strategy but reducing my options to all or nothing generally raised the stakes of losing to the point where I overprepared and became highly efficient in pursuing my goals.

Despite my track record, I think it is also important to have a Plan B. My decision to apply only to UCT seemed reckless, but I knew there were several South African universities that would accept walk-in applications. I could make my plan work from there.

In terms of the character I have become, this has worked for me in many ways. It is possible to achieve your intended outcome through a different route. There is never a permanent blockage to your destination. I could have gone back and repeated matric to make sure I got into business science, but I decided instead to evaluate my options for getting into the graduate programmes of the companies I had targeted, through a parallel route.

It's important to work with what you have and to be well rounded because there's more to life than one subject. You're at your best when you're you, so play to your strengths rather than trying to turn weaknesses into strengths.

Reaching university was humbling for me, not least because I was now far away from home. This was actually a deliberate strategy – I had always wondered whether I had done well enough at school to skip a grade because I was the son of a school principal and received extra tutoring. I tended to get what I wanted and was treated with kid gloves by my community. I needed to see whether I could stand on my own. Was I good enough?

UCT was the deep end. Nobody could come defend me. Despite having visited Brazil, not even my father had been to Cape Town before. It was expensive to fly me there, so when I left for university I was on my own, getting on a plane for the first time with nothing more than the name of my university residence on a piece of paper to direct the taxi driver. I knew my real life would begin once I got to the airport.

This was before mobile phones, which meant, at the age of 15, my connection with Gazankulu was a pay phone in a corridor of my residence. I was worried about my readiness, but one of the most incredible chance happenings was befriending the head student of my residence, Mavuso Shabalala, who was protective of me.

Each residence had a house committee with a head student and various other student body portfolios. I was, of course, the youngest student in the residence by some margin and I wondered if there had been an administrative error – I was somehow placed in a mixed-gender residence that was typically allocated to more mature students.

I felt fortunate that Mavuso took a liking to me and we quickly became friends. I was surprised when he suggested that I stand for the house committee in elections, which took place in September of each year. He was about to step down as head student.

I had no experience, had never had a leadership position in school, had never been a prefect, had never even captained a sports team. I lacked all credentials and hadn't even considered standing, but Mavuso explained that it would be good for my career and that he had all the experience necessary to guide me through the campaigning process. This was to prove a significant lesson in taking risks and realising that experience is not everything.

Mavuso made the point that, if I failed to get elected in that year, I would have lost nothing – but would have gained experience and be better prepared for the next year. With his support and guidance, I won the portfolio by a landslide and was forced to discover aspects of my character I had never encountered before. I had to lead.

I'd enjoyed the debating and campaigning, and had a newfound sense of confidence. I was becoming a well-rounded person outside of academia – like the real me was beginning to emerge. Much as my parents had been amazing to me, I lacked the confidence that I could own everything I had achieved because I was never sure why I was succeeding. Now I had to fight my insecurities, and I was beginning to taste victory.

Among my insecurities was my race. In those days there were very few black students at UCT. I had gone from being privileged back in the homeland to being underprivileged in the real South Africa. I didn't speak English with a Model C-school accent. I didn't have the best grades. I hadn't gone to a well-recognised school. I had to fight for recognition. I was also interacting with white people for the first time.

My experience of white people until that point had been at a distance when we went to Nelspruit, now Mbombela, to buy stock for the family shop. In Gazankulu, the principal of the high school and the English and Afrikaans teachers were white. For the school to be seen as the best in the homeland it needed to attract and import teachers from better schools. To do so, white teachers were paid a danger allowance to come live in Giyani and teach us.

There were a few white civil servants such as engineers and town planners who had skills that also needed to be 'imported', and they were all paid a premium. Embarrassingly, I would also – many years later – become the recipient of such an allowance when I was sent by Diageo to work in Uganda. The salaries of foreign expatriate executives were boosted by up to 50 per cent, depending on country of origin, to tolerate living in a city with what were considered sub-par amenities and a higher risk to personal safety.

Suddenly I was in the same class as white students and I got a thrill from achieving better grades. It proved my self-worth because I am a very competitive person. I learnt that if you ever feel like you have been passed over or have missed out on something, it does not mean you can't catch up.

Though I had interacted with people of other races in Gazankulu before, such as Afrikaans teachers and farmers and Indian managers of wholesale outlets, arriving in Cape Town I found a sea of white faces – especially at UCT. The dynamics behind segregation on campus were obvious: there were points rankings, and because the education of black pupils from homelands was not as good as those of our white counterparts who had attended private schools, there tended to be a separation between the humanities and arts degrees, which were much more mixed, and the technical streams such as engineering, which were nearly completely white.

The separation rooted in historical divides was reinforced by the university's tendency to place children of ex-UCT graduates in the same residences where their parents had stayed. Certain residences were therefore completely white.

More separation ran down social clusters, including sports. Black students were comfortable playing soccer, but white students played everything else, like cricket and rugby.

Finally, if I ever visited the student financial support office, it would be full of black students – many of whom could not really afford to be at the university. When black students struggled academically and lost their bursary support, that was it – they were kicked out.

Lacking natural points of connection, I remained fascinated by how some black students enjoyed greater integration and status because of their accents, dress or lifestyles. I remember clearly that there were only two black students at UCT who had cars. Most white students had a car and a computer, but for black students it was very uncommon. The wealth gap was clear and for the first time I became politically conscious. I realised that the best of what was available in the homeland was not up to the average enjoyed by white students. I had renewed determination to compete against this external benchmark.

At the same time, however, being closer to my white peers – through social interactions, church, or residence dining halls – my eyes were opened to the fact that white people as individuals were not bad and I needn't be quite so guarded. It was the system that was bad.

We can't all come from the same background. A lack of parity meant I needed to work harder and find smart ways to catch up and overtake my more privileged counterparts. I started to push myself, and each year at UCT my grades improved on average and I let my academic achievements do the talking. I was able to free myself from intimidation and I built my confidence.

We should undertake to learn from each other and appreciate that diversity makes us stronger. Reciprocity is key because I cannot give if someone is not willing to give back. If we don't connect, no hard feelings – I guard my good relationships jealously, regardless of the other person's background.

While I was rethinking my perceptions of the gap between me and my white peers, I was also trying to overcome the intimidation I felt as a first-year student campaigning to be appointed to the house committee. I didn't feel like I qualified to be on the house committee because I thought the precursor to reaching that level was everything I had done before – that previous leadership positions would be provide natural progression onto a student body. I discovered it was possible to become a student leader without a track record.

Sometimes we can be held back by restricting our ambitions to what we have achieved in the past. If you have an innate ability to do something but have never had the opportunity to take it forward, it's never too late. Your past does not define you.

The other realisation was that sometimes listening to those who believe in us is valuable. I told Mavuso I wasn't ready for the role, but he said he had seen me in action and thought I could do it. I listened, and I believed, which overcame my self-doubt.

This was an important lesson in keeping the right company and surrounding myself with people who push and encourage me. These days, my wife frequently plays this role for me, and sometimes I do the same for her. We may not always see what we have inside us, so don't ignore messages from the company you keep.

I had to juggle my academic schedule with the house committee demands, but I came to realise I also needed a part-time job. I had been told that work experience was important to getting hired as a graduate, and I had initially been dismissive of this idea because I had grown up in a business and had worked for many years – and was still doing so during vacations.

However, I realised that being employed by my parents would never be seen as properly competitive work experience, so I decided to scout for part-time work and was attracted by Edgars providing a 30 per cent discount to staff members. They also paid weekly, in cash.

Edgars was looking for casuals and – as part of my natural propensity towards overpreparation – I approached the UCT careers office to help me with mock interviews and advice. I passed the interview and Ferdi Engelbrecht became my first-ever boss. He was the sales manager in the menswear department, and I began as sales assistant in casualwear at the age of 17. I worked Friday afternoons, and Saturday and Sunday shifts, paid at the end of each Saturday shift.

When I worked at Edgars under the management of Ferdi Engelbrecht, a gay white man, he embraced me as the only black person in his team. Ferdi respected my intellect and my ideas. Back in the homeland, being openly gay would have been frowned upon. I was being trained to work with diversity, which prepared me for the multiracial and multicultural South African corporate workplace.

Even today, this formative experience in sales remains important to me and I still talk about it regularly. Working at Edgars gave me an opportunity to see the theory I had been learning at university in practice, and I learnt a lot from the job.

One of the important lessons was in managing difficult relationships. I found myself working alongside people who had a matric qualification or less and who were full-time employees and being paid less per hour than I was as a part-time casual worker. In the canteen there was no shortage of gossip.

We were incentivised beyond our basic pay to reach targets, and I would push as hard as I could because I was and am still driven by objectives. I needed to build relationships with my colleagues and line manager, and I quickly began earning a decent amount of money.

I hadn't applied for a bursary and withheld information about this job from my parents at first, so I was able to enjoy the small pleasures of fast food, beer and entertainment on my own dime over and above my monthly allowance. My salary eventually covered a television for my room, a music system and clothing, which I felt was a huge achievement. I would even buy clothes for my friends at 30 per cent discount if they gave me the money, building up goodwill with my classmates.

It was a definitive time for me – I was learning to become convincing as a salesperson, and I got a lot more out of the job than I bargained for. In the end, Ferdi wanted me to join the Edgars graduate programme, but I was set on moving to Johannesburg when I graduated – the vibrant economic hub of the country where all the major companies were headquartered, so I could benchmark myself against the best.

Taking on the part-time job taught me that I can find extra capacity if I need to. While other students were socialising or catching up on their studies over weekends, I was working for up to 28 hours a weekend at my job. I still had to run my house committee portfolio and complete my academic assignments. I got a lot done by using the people around me, pulling in favours. I wasn't afraid to take on more responsibility.

When faced with heavy demands, it is possible to find more in yourself to deliver – to become creative and prioritise efficiently. Throughout my career I have been able to get a lot done in less time because I never run away from a challenge. When faced with too much to do and a tight deadline, I am forced to prioritise, and this skill has served me well in my career.

I wanted to take on all these roles without dropping any balls, and this was built on my foundation in the family business during my school years. Successful people work hard – it's as simple as that. If you don't tap into your extra capacity, you will remain average.

I was also not put off by holding down what could be considered a menial job. When my fellow students came to buy clothes, they found me working at Edgars over weekends. Any job matters, and I didn't consider it to be beneath me. To be a great manager you need to grow your way to the top, understanding what other employees do.

It is impossible to gain the support and respect of employees below you in an organisation without establishing relationships with them. A cornerstone of everything I have achieved in my career has been starting out as a sales representative – visiting customers, picking up damages, writing credit notes, merchandising shelves and so on. Looking back, it would have been easy to become dispirited – I hadn't studied for years to do such tasks – but I am grateful because I now understand the whole value chain.

Years later, a major reason I was promoted quickly was my ability to create sales and marketing promotions with sales reps in mind – promotions whose simplicity and effectiveness they could all understand.

Despite gaining such learnings and experience, at a certain point I became envious of fellow students who had bursaries. For those of us from backgrounds deemed historically disadvantaged, there was a lot of money washing around for use by deserving black students. I didn't qualify on the grounds of inability to pay fees, so I didn't get one, but I started wondering if it was too late to gain access to similar benefits.

There were lots of donor institutions attempting to address funding inequality, and it turned out that bursaries could be given for academic achievements during our studies. My younger brother was about to complete his matric, so I applied for a bursary on the basis of academic merit through the financial aid office and was able to surprise my parents with a 25 per cent reduction of my university fees in my final year.

I worked hard to meet the requirements, and I remember the smiles on their faces when they realised their financial burden was reduced. I felt like a grown-up. I was excited to be taking the initiative, showing responsibility. I was also aware that, with the advent of democracy in South Africa in 1994, the homeland system and its politicians were now sorely out of favour.

My father's career fortunes changed, and he had learnt a painful lesson in 1988 when the shop was burnt down because he had not been properly insured. He had to fund the rebuilding of the business from his savings; barely four years later the homeland system was disbanded, so he lost his parliament job.

At some point the business had also taken a knock after being rebuilt – boycotted by people protesting against former homeland leaders and their associates. The community was told not to buy from us, and revenue slowed to a trickle for some months. I am surprised the business survived and still exists today.

The combination of my earnings from Edgars and the bursary allowed me to be less demanding of my parents' money, and I began to think about my role in the family among my siblings. I realised I could be selfless so that there would be enough money for everyone to get what they needed.

I had capitalised on the available opportunities: I had got the bursary by working hard and without disadvantaging anyone else. The money was there, so why not use it? I felt proud, and it worked in my favour because getting a bursary for being academically deserving looked good on my CV.

University is about more than academics. My job was itself a classroom, and so was the house committee. The bursary was a lesson in leaving no stone unturned. I learnt early that a job description – like the status of 'student' – is simply the *minimum* of what you need to do. It is your involvement with things outside of the minimum that will set you apart and allow you to do what you love.

My four years at UCT were tremendously important for my self-confidence. I did more than survive, and found I had the capacity to do many things at the same time. An important lesson I picked up from this time was that to enjoy a career at the top in business, you don't have to be the *best* at everything.

A lot of my peers were individually better than I was at academia, sports or debate, but I was consistently good across a range of things. When I look at executive directors of listed companies, many didn't necessarily top their classes in one aspect, but have a broad array of skills.

Getting the bursary for academic achievement, rather than from a company, gave me freedom to apply to any graduate programme, which was exciting. It was my first real job hunt and I wanted to be a trainee manager. Typically, graduate programmes allowed you to transition from student to a managerial role quickly, though there were no guarantees and you had to meet your key performance indicators.

I needed to decide where I would receive the best training, where all the best students wanted to go, and which programmes were most difficult to get into. The feedback was unanimous – in the fast-moving consumer goods sector, the only two credible options were Unilever and P&G, which are two of the world's largest household personal care and consumer goods companies.

Both companies have a lot of products in the average supermarket. P&G is indisputably the company that developed the concept of brand management, and dominates nearly every category in which it competes, from laundry detergents to haircare and baby care. Brands and products such as Ariel, Pantene, Gillette and Pampers make P&G one of the most sought-after employers globally.

Unilever is P&G's most significant rival globally and plays in many of the same categories, with brands like Skip, Omo and Dove, but also boasts a huge foods business with household names such as Knorr and Robertson's.

I don't like spreading myself too thinly, so I generally decide what I want and then put everything into working towards those goals. I applied for three graduate programmes – some of my peers applied for many more – and was ultimately given three job offers and had to go back and decide which to accept.

I wanted to benchmark against the best, as had become my habit. Though P&G was the larger business globally and was well known for its outstanding graduate programme, the company had only just re-entered South Africa when the end of apartheid had become a certainty. Its graduate programme was restricted to seven spaces in its second-ever intake.

Unilever was taking by far the highest number of graduates – nearly ten times as many students as the P&G programme. I targeted P&G as my first choice because it was harder to get into. It would say more about me if I got in, I thought. And the company was bigger globally – I wanted to be with the best. As a clincher, I knew someone who had got into P&G and was raving about it. Unilever was my backup plan, with FNB an unlikely contender.

I had enjoyed FNB's presentations to students at UCT and applied for their graduate programme too, as a Plan B. I had no real experience in banking, but believed banks paid well and they made a good case for their graduate programme.

It is difficult to believe the context of that time – in those days there were more jobs than graduates, and companies actively competed for top achievers. Today, I meet many graduates from good universities who just cannot find jobs.

In preparation, I went to mock interviews with the careers office, spoke to people who had been interviewed by those companies, and did as much research about the companies as possible. I remember the P&G CEO came to give a lecture to the business science class and although I wasn't in that group, I bulldozed my way in and asked some questions, which helped me prepare.

I wanted to increase my chances with Unilever in a similar way. I suspected the people who came to lecture would not do so blindly – they would look at who was asking questions or giving intelligent answers, would take our names and tell recruiters to look out for us. I knew I needed to give myself a chance.

Unilever ran an annual two-week business simulation course during the mid-year vacation – the Unilever Business Case. They'd come to universities, recruit students, give them a real business situation to analyse and then require a presentation of solutions to leadership. It wasn't a job interview per se, but it was certainly a way of assessing innovative ideas from students from real-world case studies.

I was among 20 students selected, and four groups of five – each with a Unilever mentor – decamped to a hotel in Sea Point to come up with a launch strategy for the Dove cream bar in South Africa. We presented to the marketing director and CEO on the last day, and my team had the winning case study. It was exciting to be working on a real business case.

The choice was less clear-cut than I had imagined. It was easy to say no to FNB because it was a distant third choice, but Unilever offered the most money and I had enjoyed the case study experience. When I told Unilever I was going with P&G, they didn't take it lying down – I was flown to Durban to meet with senior managers.

I was wined and dined, I had a suite at the Royal Hotel, I was taken to the Elida Ponds factory and told my graduate role could be transferred to Johannesburg to suit my desires. They even raised the salary offer further. I felt special but, ultimately, saying yes to Unilever felt like going with the crowd – the appeal of P&G was that there were so few graduates. We would surely get lots of attention and responsibility and handle *real* work.

In the end, P&G just made more sense to me and, looking back, I have no regrets. The graduate programme setup was really about competition, and I had to find ways to increase my chances of getting noticed. I had been told that the business simulation with Unilever and the P&G CEO's lecture were not innocent setups, and while other students dismissed the mock interviews and case studies as a waste of time, I thought I would be remembered for going through with them. And I was.

It's no different from applying for a tender, a franchise or a job – it requires lots of preparation, and taking the same route as everyone else gets you lost in the crowd. Soccer players know this: whether it is a radical haircut or red boots, it's important to not be just another number. You don't need gimmicks, but you do need something special and different in a competitive environment.

The preparation paid off. In interviews I demonstrated an interest in the companies, asked questions, showed I could offer something. Business is a two-way street – it wasn't only the companies putting on a presentation for students.

I had achieved more than I thought possible through university, and now I felt I was ready to take on South Africa's most daunting and notorious city in my first real job. I was to develop an addiction to a fast-paced lifestyle that almost derailed my career ambitions.

3

ON THE ROAD: HOW I GOT LOST AND FOUND MY WAY BACK

After enjoying almost two months' holiday at the end of my university studies, I had a definite start date for my career: 15 January 1996. I attended graduation for my postgraduate diploma in marketing management at UCT with my parents in December and had a really good time celebrating that Christmas period.

I'd just turned 19 and my parents decided that, despite my experience of being on my own at boarding school and university, I was still too young and irresponsible to live on my own in Johannesburg. Given the city's notoriety for crime, they decided the safest place for me to live was with my mom's younger brother, who had lived and worked in Joburg for most of his adult life.

My uncle and his wife lived in Pimville, Soweto, and I showed up at their door on the Saturday before I was due to start work at P&G, which was all the way across town in Kempton Park. They didn't have children, so I became a reluctant adult child in their house, with my parents intending that I should have all my expenses covered while I was shown the ropes of the big city.

That Monday we took a taxi to Isando, which required my uncle to take a day off work, and I walked into the P&G headquarters to find two other members of the graduate trainee programme in the sales management intake – Mangi Mudau and Jason Church. A striking memory was walking up to the building past three brand new VW Jetta CLX 1.8 cars out front – white, blue and red.

I hadn't realised I was going to get a company car as part of my working tools. My uncle, though he lived in a nice house in Pimville, did not have a car. P&G was organised, and we were set up from day one. After a day of being introduced to the first cohort of graduates and arranging a buddy system for orientation, I was handed the keys to drive back to my uncle's house, more than 50 km away.

What a drive that was. I left work at about 5:30 p.m. and arrived at my uncle's a little after 9 p.m. I got lost many times, finding myself caught in central Johannesburg's gridlock. I knew how to drive from doing deliveries for the family business at an early age, but I had never been on the loose in a busy city and I wasn't good at reading maps. I was also fearful of Soweto's reputation for violence and hijackings. Eventually I stopped at a petrol station and called my uncle's house – the second attempt at telephonic directions – and he took another taxi to come get me.

The next day I drove to the office alone and I got lost again, arriving late. I didn't realise it then, but being handed the keys to a car – and getting horribly lost – was to be a metaphor for my first year in Joburg.

Our first week on the job consisted of orientation, such as the basics of sales, and in week two we met customers. Again, I felt like I'd been thrown into the deep end. We were handed a route list, customer record books and a roster of customers to start serving. By 1 February we were completely on our own with our route lists, map books, customer details and sales targets.

The only time we were physically in the P&G office was on Fridays from midday to 3 p.m., when we'd hold our weekly meetings to submit records, review and plan. The setup was quite competitive, and that's the reality of corporate life – you find yourself having to work with people who will grow at different paces. They might work against you to try to get ahead, or you could excel and leap ahead of people who have more experience.

Dealing with these dynamics can be extremely difficult and requires focus. Almost immediately after starting work I found that my wheels began to drift across the road, so to speak. I had worked hard at university, including at my part-time job, and I felt like I was now getting to enjoy the rewards of my hard work. I had a nice car and a company petrol card, I had money and no expenses, and I was one of the few black students who finished a degree without having to repay a loan.

My uncle refused my offers to contribute to anything. I had a petrol card and company car, at no cost to me. All the money I earned came straight to me as disposable income. I partied hard, all over the city. I lived the life I couldn't afford at UCT. At the time, Yeoville was the place to be, with Hillbrow and the CBD also offering up a lot of attractions for a young man with money to burn.

My uncle saved my reputation by not telling my parents what I was up to, partly because we developed a symbiotic relationship: I provided mobility whenever he wanted to go out, and he looked the other way when my social life blew up.

I wanted my hard work from my university days to pay off, not realising that this was just another phase requiring application and commitment. Unlike at university, there were no regular grades or exams to show me whether I was on track or not. I was an Average Joe, doing enough to not get fired, not realising how competitive the workplace actually was. I was thoroughly complacent.

By the middle of 1996 I'd had enough of living under someone else's roof – I found it restrictive and used the excuse that I was not comfortable driving back to Pimville late at night over weekends. I told my uncle I felt vulnerable, but in truth wanted the freedom to do things I couldn't do at his house.

A chance meeting with Mpho Maile, through a mutual friend, connected me with someone who was in exactly the same situation. Mpho was a Wits University engineering graduate and his parents had told him to stay in Pretoria with his sister while he was working for Highveld Steel in Witbank.

We decided to club together to buy furnishings and pay the rent on a townhouse in Edenvale, moving in as two young men with no loan repayments, two Jettas and the bright lights glowing invitingly before us. Now that we were fully independent, the partying escalated to a dizzying level. I don't remember much about that year, other than taking my first international trip to Belgium for sales training at the impressive P&G global academy.

At work, I was cutting corners. Once I became familiar with some customers, I wouldn't go to see them any more. I was one of the first people to have a company mobile phone so I would call my customers and take their orders, or check on them without visiting my area, which was the East Rand. I considered some customers, like those in Springs, to be simply too far away for me to drive to.

Of course, it all caught up with me. My line manager would make unannounced visits to customers and knew what to look out for – the outlets would be in bad shape, volumes were not coming through, the merchandising wasn't up to scratch. I'd be handed demerit points, which characterised my whole first year at work.

At the end of our first year we were given our annual reviews, and my 360-degree review was a painful wake-up call for me. I had joined the sales stream of the graduate programme with Mangi and Jason, but Mangi was older than us because he'd been a teacher and had gone back to do a BCom to switch careers. He was very focused and professional, while Jason had been disciplined.

The other two were adjudged to have delivered much better results and were promoted to the second rotation of the programme, while my assessment said I hadn't done enough. Until I ticked all the boxes for the first year I would be held back.

I was disappointed and suddenly able to see the tangible result of my failure to apply myself to my work properly. I was given six months to improve, or I would be shipped out as what P&G called a 'recruitment error' – a term reserved for people who had somehow played the system and were usually professional test-takers who knew how to get into companies but then failed to perform. It was a horrifying prospect for me.

Failing to progress to the second phase of the graduate trainee programme also meant I didn't get a salary increase or an even better car, while my colleagues did. I was still a business development representative while they were now handling district field representative duties, working on key accounts.

I started isolating myself from my fellow graduates, feeling like I'd lost my friends. My response was to change my lifestyle: I didn't go out as much, I tried to grow up and stabilise myself. Mpho had a similarly rough review at work. We both knew our careers may be over before they had really begun.

Feeling stung, I worked harder. I was given a new region to cover, and I exceeded my targets. Despite my earlier revelations about working so-called menial jobs while I was Edgars, I had to fix my attitude towards my job – though I considered myself a humble person, I had developed a complex about working as a sales rep.

While my old university mates were now doing articles at accounting firms or walking around in suits, I was having my pants stained by broken bleach bottles I was collecting from retail outlets. To me, there was an embarrassment factor that came with having a degree and being called to collect damaged packets of Pampers.

I didn't feel proud of the job I was doing, but with hindsight it was another great learning experience – that's where sales happen. Everything I was doing was driving revenue for the company. Whatever market share P&G had in my area was under my control. Whichever customer relationships, complaints and requirements came out of my area – all were under *my* control. I was the one who was responsible for making P&G relevant for customers in my area.

I dusted myself off and my appreciation of the job began to increase. By May I was promoted to the second rotation and by November I was promoted again to the third and final rotation, ahead of my two peers.

I had been provoked. I had been shown up as a non-performer and I was angry. The key to making such an adjustment is recognising when things have gone wrong. Sometimes it can be difficult to discern when we aren't fully committed or our jobs have lost our attention, but it's important to realise that nothing is lost forever. A wake-up call can be embraced – we just have to find our way back.

Corporate organisations can be quite forgiving. You can prove yourself if you show that the mistake was a blip, a temporary setback. I learnt to balance the bright lights of Joburg with competing at work. I restored my pride and let go of my distractions, getting back to the person I knew I was.

I was trying to repay P&G for the faith it had in me, which was my inspiration for rediscovering my work ethic. I remembered that I wanted to be a CEO, and I was fascinated by people who ran companies – not least by Roberto Marinucci, who had come from P&G in Italy to establish the company's brands in this country.

It was motivating to watch him in action. Others at P&G had more experience in the South African market than he did – especially since Permark International had bought some of the P&G distribution licences when P&G left the country during apartheid. They were big personalities who were good at what they did.

Roberto was also young, in his early thirties, and clearly less experienced than some of the brand executives. But he led with a lot of flair and treated everyone with respect. He was very calm and intellectual, and it's no surprise that he went on to become one of the company's global vice-presidents in later years. I learnt that you don't have to be the oldest to be the wisest – you can lead people who are more experienced than you are.

I also learnt that Roberto didn't have to be the most charismatic or the loudest talker in the room to be the leader. By contrast, Paul Fray was sales director for P&G in South Africa and he was charisma personified – very persuasive, very energetic and extremely sharp.

Paul's job was to create market share for P&G products from zero, and in categories where P&G had entrenched competition or copycats. I watched him in action and learnt presentation skills: articulation, being able to convince people to adopt something, creating excitement. He was incredible at these skills.

At the time, P&G was still developing its structures in South Africa and the twenty or so graduates from two years of intakes were operating in a very flat hierarchy. It was an exciting time to be there, and we had direct access to senior leaders, only one of whom was South African.

Globally, P&G's strategy is to promote from within, so we received a lot of attention. We represented the company's first hires in South Africa, and the system believed in graduates. Our responsibilities were accelerated because our leaders had also started out as graduates. A year in this programme was, I believe, about the equivalent of two years in another fast-moving consumer goods (FMCG) company's programme. I was involved in 19 product launches in 5 years.

The small staff complement meant we took part in everything. We worked long hours and did more than we were paid for. In later years I became cynical of interview processes where companies focused too much on what was on a CV. No two people experience 12 months in the same way. If I've achieved twice as much as someone else in that time, do we have the same amount of experience? Time matters, but content and output matter more.

We were doing things other graduates wouldn't get to do, even by global standards, because we were building P&G's presence from scratch. We were sales reps, but we were also putting in hours on accounts, launches and strategy. If I were to do it all again, I'd still choose P&G.

In my second rotation I was pushed hard, working for a Dutch line manager, Herman Holtus. He had been headhunted by Paul Fray to establish a customer marketing capability in South Africa as a revered expert in the field. He went on to become CEO of one of the world's largest chocolatiers, and I had the privilege of working for him in his younger days.

What a line manager! As far as I am concerned, he is still the gold standard in line management: he was really energetic, hardworking, and the thing about him that few other line managers ever master is that he empowered his people. His favourite words were, 'I trust you.'

He took risks on us, transferring responsibility. We dared not disappoint. Herman also acted in an entirely authentic way. I'd heard before that the Dutch are a direct people, but Herman seemed to take this to another level. He would show you the required standard and showcase himself as a role model, and then be incredibly direct about what he expected and how you performed.

If you had to present to someone senior allowed into that forum, he would let you set up your own presentation, no matter how junior you were. He would step in to help where necessary, but mostly you were allowed to take over. I'd never encountered a line manager who was so unthreatened.

In short, we were allowed to shine so that when he left, we could be promoted. I've tried to uphold the same philosophy – to selflessly develop and grow team members and give them the exposure they need. Reporting to Herman, I went from knowing nothing about customer marketing to heading health and beauty care – a smaller segment than many in the P&G stable, but the most profitable.

Under his guidance I really grew to understand retail and was in tune with my customers. We did a lot of international benchmarking. It was a growth period for me, and I was having fun.

The thing about not doing well at work is that it can be a self-fuelling cycle – you can become demotivated. If you don't arrest the slide and turn it around, you become depressed and begin to put in even less effort, which leads to a spiralling lack of rewards.

I've learnt to seek feedback constantly and to take ratings seriously. Career development plans are not simply tick-box exercises. If the tools are there, use them. As much as success breeds success, failure begets failure. Potential can't be fulfilled without the confidence bred by success.

Herman's feedback could be brutal, but it was effective because it was honest. I remember when he had trusted me with a particular presentation to Roberto, where we sought support for a strategy, and it didn't go well. Frankly, I lost confidence during preparation and hadn't sought enough input from Herman. We were torn apart and we deserved to be.

Herman, a competitive person, was extremely disappointed. Though he tried to maintain a united front by supporting me in front of Roberto, he couldn't rescue the situation. When I later followed Herman back to his office he closed the door and delivered his judgement: 'Nyimpini, that was shit and you know it.' Herman didn't sugar-coat anything, but I needed to hear it.

He told me he knew I could do better, and that I'd let myself down. It was true, and these things happen – not every day will be a good day. The key is recovery. Even as CEOs we haven't become perfect – meetings and presentations won't always go well, and we must find our way back. It helps nobody if the feedback isn't honest, though it should also be constructive.

Being self-critical is an important part of growing, as is appreciating that you're always in competition with others. There can be only one CEO of a company at any one time. You need to learn how to help yourself if you want to make it happen. Deliver strong results if you can, and know where you stand if you can't. I learnt such lessons working for leaders like Herman.

After nine months of working with him I was approached by the new CEO of P&G South Africa, Paul Hart. Roberto had moved on to take over as CEO in Egypt, a much larger market, and Paul's job was to execute the second phase of P&G's entrenchment in the South African marketplace.

The reason behind Paul's approaching me was that Roberto had established a cash van project before his departure. This project was interesting because it was P&G's attempt to penetrate the informal township retail market to grow distribution. At the time, in the late nineties, many companies sought a foothold in these markets through cash-and-carry wholesalers from which the spaza shops and superettes bought their stock.

Metro was the largest cash-and-carry player, and they also owned a chain called Trade Centre. The role of the wholesaler was to buy in bulk, because distributing to the last mile in the townships was a logistical challenge and businesses were afraid to tackle it. It was a very passive model of distribution from the periphery of a township.

Metro enjoyed a near-monopoly at the time, controlling some 80 per cent of the wholesale market. With that came a degree of arrogance – if you wanted your products on Metro's shelves, you had to do it on their terms. P&G had tried to negotiate listings into Metro, but Metro required a R1 million payment just to allow products in, with monthly promotional spend and our own shelf organisation needed on top of that. We considered these abusive terms, and we could develop no relationships with actual traders.

Roberto said he'd rather spend the money trying to reach informal retailers directly, which was a bold move. Many larger competitors in South Africa, like Nestlé and Unilever, had not attempted that. Those who did, such as Coca-Cola and the milk and bread brands, still listed at Metro for replenishment because their frequency of calling at retailers was low.

The model Roberto followed came from successful operations in Poland and Egypt, where vans would pick up products and sell into convenience channels daily. Some Polish nationals were brought to South Africa and P&G found a local partner for the establishment of a new business unit, to be led by Isaac Chalumbira.

This was a good localisation story years before BEE came into play. The distribution model was adapted for South African conditions and perfected over six months of trial runs, and then it launched. However, after roughly six months of operating, the business ran into problems and was shut again.

Isaac left armed with learnings from the project and was headhunted by Coca-Cola to work in their sales department in a senior position. The pioneering and innovative setup for going deeper into townships had caught Coca-Cola's attention and was later refined in a way that suited fast-moving goods like soft drinks.

P&G had lost money but decided that it wanted to try again. Paul wanted to follow a model that was more Egyptian than Polish, to reduce costs and cover the right geography. He also wanted the product portfolio changed to carry faster-moving items. This was to be a joint venture. P&G brought in a township activation partner, part of the Primedia Group, which was another black-empowered entity.

Non-competing partners were brought in to optimise basket size and van capacity, and some expatriate managers were brought in to assist for the first six months. The second incarnation of the cash van project got off the ground with 19 vans in Gauteng, Mpumalanga and KwaZulu-Natal.

Paul asked me to head up the cash van operation when the foreign nationals left. I was terrified. At 21 I had just two years of corporate experience and was being asked to run an operation across three provinces. Each van was operated by two people, and we shared warehouse space with Primedia in Jet Park, so, including financial and administration staff, this meant leading a team of about fifty people.

My first line manager at P&G, in my first graduate programme rotation, had been Ashley Langa. I had been in charge of the East Rand and Ashley was sales supervisor for Gauteng East and South. Two years later, I became his boss since Ashley was now a supervisor for the cash van operation. This was to become my next significant challenge and lesson: managing someone who had formerly been my superior.

I respected Ashley and he'd taught me how to do my first job, so I had no idea how I might manage or even possibly reprimand my former mentor. I might be the one who had to decide whether to promote or fire Ashley.

I was afraid to accept the offer, not least because I knew the cash van operation had failed before, even when run by the hugely capable Isaac. Failure could signal the end of my career at P&G.

I decided to counter my self-doubt by listening to those who believed in me, which Paul did. I am naturally a risk taker and thrive on being challenged. Even though a R15 million investment into cash vans in 1997 was a lot of money, I accepted because I thought I had no option but to make it work. If I was to fulfil my ambition of being a CEO, I needed to take the opportunity to run a business for the first time.

My targets and deadline for when we had to break even were clear. I had to find a way to make the unit profitable, so it was a true end-to-end role.

I travelled to the satellite warehouse in Mbombela and to our KwaZulu-Natal offices regularly. My channel head, Elizabeth Stenhauser, was another of the P&G archetypes because she was super-bright and astute, but the cash van project was a different animal from any she'd encountered before, and I was largely left to my own devices.

I had to learn fast while trying to add value to the business. How could I bring fresh thinking and innovation to a model that was practically unknown? I couldn't replicate any South African best practice to make it work.

After a quick handover, I literally got into the vans to see how they ran. One of my strengths is building relationships, so I wanted to experience what the van operators were experiencing. I needed to see their daily routines, their challenges, their risks. I didn't want to be shielded from anything.

The most exciting part of this role was building customer relationships, seeing them appreciative of deliveries when they had run out of stock. Now they didn't have to leave their shops to replenish.

Many of my learnings from servicing the cash van customers remain applicable to my job today. I had to figure out how to reduce costs, and Ashley and I enjoyed a fruitful relationship in strategising. He was humble and supportive, and I valued his contribution to my learnings. You have to learn from the people you manage.

Another part of the job I enjoyed was interacting with the Kirsch family, owners of Primedia, who were now part of the board to whom I reported. We'd meet for dinner and build our relationship, which meant I was being exposed to a great corporate in P&G but also to true entrepreneurs at Primedia.

Being aware that there are other routes to the top office than those within corporates has defined my career. I chose P&G when they were barely in the country and were not a fashionable option.

At P&G, most of my fellow graduates wanted to work in the largest and most attractive portfolios where they could travel and work key accounts with large retail groups, because P&G had practically invented brand management. In that light, cash van sales seemed like career suicide: there was no next step to other territories, or anything like the same recognition.

I was ambitious, but I was more interested in the maverick side of business – I was excited about doing something different, about taking the road less travelled. You can still make it to CEO level on the regular route, but I believe CEOs and other executives need to create, and that calls for disruption. It means taking risks and doing things differently. Again, I wanted to stand out from the crowd.

For me to win, the company must win. When all is said and done, my salary is a cost, so I needed to focus on value creation. The more I ran the cash vans business and focused on targets, the more I began to wonder how we could do it better.

At the time, it seemed like a lot of effort for small wins, but they became more significant when Metro realised we were gaining traction. If we proved that the formula could work, other FMCG companies might further cannibalise the cash-and-carry model. Metro approached P&G and said they would waive the R1 million listing fee, and relax other trading terms.

With that offer on the table, I realised we could continue slogging ahead with just 19 vans in three provinces or we could gain instant scale through Metro and eliminate the overheads that were part of the cash van operating model. Unprompted, I walked into Paul's office and did something I've done many times in my career – I surprised the CEO with a bold recommendation that we close the cash van project.

Paul couldn't believe his ears, but I told him I'd looked at the numbers and knew that if we didn't close it, we'd lose R5 million. If we went with Metro, we'd make a handsome profit. Paul had a finance background and I showed him we were sitting on a ticking time bomb, even though we were still on track from an operational standpoint. Many of our previous assumptions were flawed, so we needed to avoid paying the opportunity cost at Metro.

He had to go back to his bosses in London and convince them the project he'd been tasked with reviving needed to be shut down. The numbers spoke for themselves and the decision was made, though it came as a shock while morale in the cash van operation was still running high.

Primedia took the news badly, but I was promoted at P&G and received an award recognising me for making the tough call to avoid losses, ultimately improving P&G's business overall. This was the pinnacle of my career so far, at the age of 23, and it came from knowing when to let go.

Many start-up businesses fail, and a key skill as a businessperson is to know when to hold on and when to quit. We all go through due diligence and hope for the best, but mistakes are sometimes made. Even global powerhouses like Wal-Mart make mistakes, if you look at their struggles with the Game brand in South Africa or the recent decision to sell their wholesale division, which includes brands like Cambridge and Jumbo, as making profit continues to be a struggle.

It can come down to something as simple as timing. Coca-Cola launched its cherry cola and Fresca brands with huge fanfare, massive marketing budgets and broad distribution, but still couldn't make them work. Withdrawing an idea is part of a CEO's competency. In wanting to show that our ideas work, we shouldn't try to spare our egos by pushing too hard and too long.

I've registered many failures, but more successes. I try to stick to the maxim that that you should fail fast and learn fast. If you fail slowly, you can lose a lot of money. We should also avoid punishing failures too severely. If teams are too afraid to take any risks, there will be no exponential learning curves and no first-mover advantage.

By electing to shut down the cash van business I was rendering myself unemployed. I was thinking of the company first, so I let them decide where and how to redeploy me. I don't know where I found the maturity to make the decision, but it served me well, even if it meant my days at P&G were effectively numbered.

I gained a lot of respect at P&G – particularly from Paul, who had dealt with me directly despite my official reporting line to Elizabeth. After we wound down the cash van business, gave our notice on properties and sold off assets, I was disappointed by the next role offered to me, as key account manager for the wholesale and convenience channel, such as Metro, Makro and service station stores. I felt I was done with direct sales and wanted a different challenge. I wanted a diversity of skills to further prepare me for a leadership role, so I enquired about a move to marketing, but nobody at P&G was thrilled about that.

This was a strongly functional company – you stayed in your lane and built your career in one function to reach director level. But that wasn't what I wanted.

When they saw I was serious they told me I'd have to take a few backward steps into a role of assistant brand manager because my experience wasn't transferable. At the same time I happened to be approached by an executive search firm who told me that they were recruiting for a marketing manager at what would be the equivalent of senior brand manager in P&G terms.

I realised that if I stayed at P&G, even though things had been going well for me, I would be held back. I was being offered a marketing management role for the largest spirit alcohol brand in the country, Smirnoff vodka, at Diageo. From my position in the sales team I marvelled at what the brand and marketing managers were doing – working closely with consumer insights and acting as the fulcrum for innovation. The marketing team held a lot of power in an organisation that was centred on brand building.

Each consumer goods category within P&G operated as a strategic business team, so baby care, feminine protection and health and beauty care would each have a trade marketing, production and finance team, headed by a marketing manager and accountable for profits and losses in the category. I knew that if I were to grow to be a general manager within the P&G environment, my brand knowledge and track record would need to be strong. I felt I had learnt enough in my role and wanted to diversify into marketing.

It was at about this time that I received the call from an executive search firm about the marketing manager role for Smirnoff at Guinness UDV (now Diageo). I didn't have the strong marketing background I thought I needed, but they told me they were aware of me and knew my profile and I'd be a good fit. This was the message I had wanted from within P&G. Again, I listened to those who had faith in me.

The role at Diageo involved a big budget and a team of brand managers and assistant brand managers, which sounded enticing and transformational for my career – but it was in Cape Town. Though I was keen on staying in Joburg, I flew down for the interviews and met everyone in one short trip. I was offered the role for more than double my P&G salary and suddenly had a decision to make.

I decided I should focus on the bigger picture and that Cape Town wouldn't be a dealbreaker, so I accepted. I had learnt much at P&G and the company had provided the foundation of my career, but I handed in my resignation after just five years.

Though there were counteroffers from P&G, on a personal level I felt my time with the company was up – particularly when Paul's attempts at getting me to stay turned sour. He ridiculed both Diageo and alcohol as a product, and focused on what P&G had done for me – rather than acknowledging the hard work I had put in for the company. After being denied an opportunity to build on my work, I felt this made the decision to leave easier, and our personal relationship ended there.

I was young, but I could see that the alcohol industry employed many people, created many entrepreneurs, paid lots of taxes and could be an exciting prospect for brand management. I met many great people at P&G and would not trade those first years for anything, but it was time to move on.

4
SOMETIMES YOU NEED TO SLOW DOWN TO GO FASTER

I returned to Cape Town at the end of 2000 to take up an opportunity with Guinness UDV, which would later become Diageo South Africa. Though I had not initially wanted to leave Johannesburg, I am thankful for my second stint in Cape Town because it gave me not only an accelerated career development curve, but also the chance to meet the lady who would become my wife.

Smirnoff was the most significant and profitable brand in Guinness UDV's largest category, white spirits, contributing about 36 per cent of the company's profit at the time and making up about half of their volume. The irony struck me: P&G, the company I had worked for and which knew my capabilities well, had been unwilling to let me step sideways into a marketing role, while a company I barely knew was willing to offer me a promotion to a position in which the brand managers of the company's most important category would be reporting to *me*.

At first, I felt they had made a mistake. I was only 23. Why were they even interested in me? Then I decided that I had absolutely nothing to lose – if they *had* made a mistake, the worst that could happen was that I'd get a free trip to Cape Town.

I flew down and met with the company's leadership over two days and had fun. I was bold and it resonated with them – I told them my ideas for the Smirnoff brand and, despite my shortcomings in experience, they must have liked the breath of fresh air. This was an important lesson: I had no direct experience but was a quick learner and had a good grounding in commerciality and the pragmatic nature of the role. I played to my strengths and didn't let my weaknesses dominate. I let my experience in P&G's largest and most profitable business unit lead, and showed that I had paid attention to what experienced marketeers did.

One week later I was made an offer that would double my salary as the marketing manager for the biggest brand in Diageo SA's portfolio. I moved to Cape Town and discovered a number of challenges waiting for me.

I was the first black marketing manager Diageo SA had hired and one of very few black leaders in the company. I was also the most senior marketing manager by portfolio and the youngest by at least five years, yet I had no direct marketing experience. I was also coming into the business from Gauteng, when nearly everyone else at the company had grown up in Cape Town or Stellenbosch. Cape Town has gained a reputation for not being welcoming to black leaders, and when I moved into Durbanville – a suburb that was almost uniformly white and Afrikaans – I learnt a lot about being out of my comfort zone.

Though the odds seemed stacked against me, this was one of my most successful assignments. I simply did not give any time to thinking about what I *didn't* have. I didn't care. I was young, naïve, ambitious and focused on delivering. What really carried me was my passion for the job and for marketing. I also found that I was able to thrive *because* of what I had that my colleagues did not. Liquor businesses tended to set up headquarters in the Western Cape because the vineyards and related agriculture was there, but it meant they didn't truly understand the Gauteng market that contributed half of all revenue. And if business leaders did visit Gauteng, they tended to restrict themselves to establishments in upmarket neighbourhoods like Sandton.

I used this to my advantage. Growth prospects did not lie in the white male market that liquor companies were still targeting. I had insights into the emerging black middle class, and the contacts and experience to make campaigns work. Rather than feel disadvantaged as a minority within the business, I found I had an edge.

Another important lesson from this time was to form partnerships for knowledge exchange. Where my colleagues lacked emerging black customer nous, I lacked detailed knowledge of the liquor industry. There is strength in unity, in sharing insights, and it worked well for me. I developed a strong relationship with Rynard van der Westhuizen, marketing manager for Bell's whisky at the time.

Rynard had been around for a long time and knew that the future of the brand lay beyond the golfing and fly-fishing hooks on which campaigns had been hung before. I wanted to know more about leading with product, leveraging sponsorships, product excellence and driving quality, and we developed a mutually beneficial relationship.

Most important to my success in Cape Town with Diageo was the belief my line manager, Mike Joubert, had in me. He took a personal and professional risk in betting on my passion and talent. My appointment raised eyebrows, including those of Mike's boss, but Mike backed me to the hilt despite my deficiencies. This was the beginning of a special relationship which endures today. Mike remains a friend and mentor.

Mike gave me decision rights, telling me that I should not wait for him if time to market was an issue. He asked only that I consider what he may have done in the same situation, knowing that eight out of ten times we'd make the same decision given the information before us.

Too often executives can delay decisions out of fear, losing crucial early mover advantage. Mike's approach was that we should act now and apologise later – within governance and risk frameworks, of course. Don't hide behind conflicting information and don't lose the advantage of speed. This has become my philosophy.

Along with the development of special relationships within Diageo, I laid the foundations for 15 years spent with the company, across seven roles and three countries. It was all started by Mike taking a liking to me. That was my break.

I was given another significant break at the beginning of 2002 when I met my future wife, Mosima, by chance at Marcel's Frozen Yoghurt on Main Road in Rondebosch. I had been visiting a friend and stopped in for a frozen yoghurt on my way home, finding Mosima keeping her friend Tumi company. Tumi was working behind the counter while Mosima sat at one of the high chairs and I was struck by her beauty, her presence, her smile and her innocence.

I don't make a habit of approaching people in shops but this time I was overcome. I went over to introduce myself and offered to buy her a tub. She later told me she'd already had two tubs but couldn't say no, and that's how we got talking. I got her number and we went on subsequent dates, where I was patient and persistent, winning her heart.

My time in Cape Town became that much more special, but it also meant I had more than my career to consider. When Mosima completed her medical studies, she needed to return to Gauteng to work and I couldn't bear the thought of being without her, so I told Diageo I had to relocate to Johannesburg and leave the business. Little did I know that two years later I would be recalled to Diageo and move to the UK.

Mosima and I were married shortly after moving back to Joburg and have been married for 15 years, blessed with two boys. I think I'm the luckiest man on Earth to have such an intelligent, hard-working and supportive wife.

When I left Diageo in 2006 I was very fortunate to be appointed as a franchise joint venture partner for the incredibly well-run and highly sought-after Nando's in the Johannesburg CBD. I thought running my own business could be my route to leadership. I had met and became friends with Robbie Brozin, co-founder and CEO of Nando's, and I found him full of inspiring business and life lessons. The opportunity to co-own and run a six-store operation as joint-venture CEO appealed to me because this was real hands-on operational experience. I was getting a taste of what I really wanted.

This was a great transformation story, not only because I was black and therefore a great B-BBEE scorecard asset for Nando's, but because all the outlets my partner and I controlled were in the city centre of Johannesburg. I was integrally involved in the process of urban renewal, which was dragging the city back from decades of urban blight.

Watching the CBD decay had been painful for me. As a rural boy, having grown up in the former Gazankulu homeland, visiting my uncle in Soweto as a high school pupil was always the highlight of my year. He would take me shopping in the Carlton Centre, one of the most prominent landmarks on the Johannesburg skyline, among other places I had only read or heard about.

My uncle's favourite clothing shops were found in Small Street, so I was very excited, many years later, to own Nando's outlets at both the Carlton Centre and in Small Street. My office was situated along with another Nando's outlet in the iconic Gandhi Square. Inner-city rejuvenation in Johannesburg had a very personal aspect for me.

The role at Nando's ticked many boxes in terms of what I sought in my professional life: I was now a CEO of a business, which was my dream job. Although I ran only 6 outlets, there were 98 staff members employed and a decent turnover of a couple of million rand along with a highly leveraged balance sheet with loans to service. I was looking for space to open more branches or acquire other franchisees to consolidate the Nando's operations in the CBD. I also nurtured a vision of opening franchises of other brands, as some successful franchisee role models I knew of had done.

Running my own business forced me to become a very efficient leader: when it's your own money you think twice before you increase your employee headcount, because those are extra salaries to pay and people's lives you don't want to disrupt if your plans don't work out.

Suddenly, I began to wonder whether a meeting in Cape Town – requiring a plane ticket, hotel stay and time away from work – was necessary. The typical justifications employed to make plane-hopping *seem* necessary as part of a natural greasing of the corporate wheels came to look wasteful to me – as much as they were prized as rewards by leaders in the corporate world.

Executives, in general, travel far too much, attend meetings and events that are unnecessary, hire luxury cars and stay in fancy hotels when they don't need to. It's always useful to compare how the same executives would choose to spend the money if it were their own. As an entrepreneur, I learnt to pare back all unnecessary expenses. I wanted to spend only on things that would contribute to growing my business and not to accept the first price I was quoted. I learnt to negotiate to get the best deal possible. I was obsessed with productivity and efficiency.

I found later that I was able to apply these learnings in a corporate environment to make myself stand out as a business leader. I discovered I had learnt an important lesson while I was involved with Nando's: not all the skills one needs to be successful in a corporate are learnt in a corporate.

For an individual to grow and be successful in a highly competitive environment, it's imperative that you bring something fresh to the situation. A perspective that stands apart from the average view of what needs to be done in a business can be a great advantage. If you don't have something unique to contribute, how else will you stand out?

The hallmark of my success in a corporate environment has been the application of an entrepreneurial mindset. I grew up in a family business and then ran my own business, and it is seldom the case that people who have tasted that life will want to try fit into a highly defined and segmented role in a corporate. Such people can make great CEOs precisely because they want to get their hands dirty running a business. Being kept away from the levers of control until that final point often frustrates true entrepreneurs into working outside such structures.

The path to the top can frustrate even those who feel comfortable in corporate environments. But few people realise that bringing unique talents from outside the workplace can contribute to success and advancement within a corporation.

If you preach in your local church, have you used that skill to deliver compelling speeches and presentations at work? If you are passionate about IT and have an idea for driving digitisation at work, have you approached the finance department about automating processes to increase efficiency and reduce costs? There are always opportunities to stand out and provide the spark for career growth.

The fundamentals of being a CEO and running your own company are the same: you hire, you fire, you make decisions, you seek funding, you try to strengthen your balance sheet, take appropriate risk and manage your key stakeholder relationships.

I dealt with a Nando's board that boasted some very powerful business leaders as shareholders, and I learnt to engage with funders who needed to be comfortable with how my business was performing and could cover interest repayments. Running a business is mostly about relationships – suppliers, staff, creditors, landlords, a whole smorgasbord of individuals and entities who become intertwined in your business operations and need to be kept happy.

Even with a brand like Nando's behind me, I was constantly thinking about revenue and expenses to avoid my dream crashing around me. I had cashed out my Diageo pension to fund the equity portion of my business, which created additional pressure to make it work – I literally had no retirement money if I were to fail. Talk about skin in the game!

In a corporate environment I have often heard the phrase 'act like an owner', or to behave with a 'founder's mindset'. This means to treat the company's assets as if they were your own in growing the business. The reason I hit the ground running when I returned to a corporate was that, by this stage, it came naturally to me after nearly two years without a safety net. My competitive edge was that I had skills no corporate position could teach.

Long before I became a CEO in a corporate, I was able to work like one and think like one – looking at the business as an interconnected and integrated system, so that I could make sustainable decisions.

I was unaware that my departure from the corporate world of Diageo into the fast-growing and entrepreneurial Nando's business had been seen as a misstep by my former managing director, Simon Litherland, who is now group CEO of Britvic plc in the UK. Simon called me 18 months later to ask if I would like to consider returning – this time to a regional role in the UK. Why would I want to re-join the corporate world where my path to becoming a CEO was not guaranteed? Put bluntly, the lure of international experience and to become CEO of a large corporate was the simple answer.

There was still a lot to think about, and the decision about how I could best advance my career was not clear-cut. I would be ending an addictive and barely realised entrepreneurial dream by going back to a corporate job, and it threw into relief exactly how much I needed to know where I was headed if I were to give up working for myself.

I had a bankable idea and funding behind me, good traction in the business and powerful shareholders who were happy with my performance. I was also, at the time, one of very few black franchisees and certainly the first black joint venture partner. That said, I was always attracted to a career with international experience. It is just my mindset — the more situations and contexts you can learn from, the broader your capability for dealing with unexpected events.

Growing up in a village in a rural homeland under apartheid frustrated me because I could not see the world. One of my most prized memories was when my late father visited Brazil in the eighties as part of the former Gazankulu homeland delegation, and shared the pictures from his trip with me.

I had a dream to be a child of the world and working for a multinational seemed like just the right fit for my ambitions. It is no coincidence that I have spent most of my career in global groups like P&G, Diageo, Boston Consulting Group, GE and Vodacom/Vodafone.

To me, South Africa's international isolation during apartheid seeped into its business outlook, so that working for a local company would not make me the best leader I could be because of a lack of global benchmarking. Besides, the companies we all recognised as South African consumers were almost always Fortune 500 players from the US.

It has always been simple, to my mind: if you want to be the best, train with the best, compete with the best. Even better, aim to beat the best.

In my quest to be the best, it was not good enough for me that, 12 years into my career, I had only worked in South Africa with occasional international trips into the bargain. The prospect of working in the UK was just too valuable to pass up. Hard as it was to say goodbye to my business and my team, who had become like family to me, it was reassuring that my wife — who at the time was four months pregnant with our first child — was extremely supportive, despite being fearful of becoming a mother without having family members around.

Stepping out of Nando's is what I call slowing down to move faster. My new role in the UK did not pay me more than I was making at Nando's, and had I stayed with the franchise the value of my investment would have grown substantially, but I have no regrets. I took a salary cut and lost a business to make sure that my future earnings would be greater — a decision that was I later vindicated in making.

I had an incredible time in the UK, despite an initial adjustment phase in the first year — especially coping with spending more than half my time travelling from the UK back to several countries in Africa. I was working in new markets, completely out of my comfort zone, meeting new people and handling brands I had never even heard of before.

The experience was beneficial for my career because there were a lot of similarities between the markets for which I was strategising and the townships in which I had lived and worked. I was familiar with the business constraints and challenges of underdeveloped infrastructure such as the lack of water and electricity; with spaza shops, the route to market and value chains. This gave me an advantage. Walking the streets with the locals at ease is something the employees and other local stakeholders saw me doing and they loved that I was such a relationship builder. I am a natural extrovert and networking comes naturally to me because I love people.

This is another important aspect of doing business with anyone: even if we disagree on matters of strategy or execution, respect and relationships need to be maintained. I was very clear about who I needed to impress and cultivate relationships with, because they were the decision makers for my next role. I knew I was constantly being assessed.

Something I learnt early on was that you should always try to understand how promotions or appointment decisions are made, and who is involved in making them. It's important to show up well to those people whenever the opportunity arises. Through both the circumstances of my new role in African markets and my own steadfast focus on cultivating the right relationships, doors were opened to me.

Working in London while serving African markets really opened my eyes. Coming from South Africa, where the top strata of listed company leaders were dominated by white males, I did not have a direct role model to look up to. I had never even met a black CEO by that point. In London I ran into black CEOs in Diageo Africa, and they were running some of the largest markets in the portfolio.

There was no shortage of examples: Gerald Mahinda was CEO of Diageo East African Breweries Limited (EABL) and was an inspirational, high-performing leader. Baker Magunda was CEO of Meta Abo Brewery in Ethiopia. Peter Ndegwa, who went on to become CEO of the Diageo European Cluster business and is now CEO of Safaricom. Ekwunife Okoli, former CEO of Africa Regional Markets. Seni Adetu, former CEO of Guinness Nigeria.

This reminded me of discovering, on a trip in 1998, that the commercial aircraft in which I was flying was captained by a black African from Kenya. I had never seen a black pilot before. It gave me hope, being surrounded by these great gentlemen who were successfully navigating their way through companies that employed so many people back in Africa.

Nick Blazquez, then president of Diageo in Africa, used to say he dreamed of a Diageo business in Africa run entirely by Africans. That inspired me and added impetus to my aspirations within the company. Most of the leaders were generous with their time when I approached them for guidance, providing helpful advice, mentorship and feedback.

I felt comfortable seeking guidance because they were doing the jobs I hoped to hold one day. I asked for their stories of how they made it to the top, which mistakes they made, who helped them, and so on. I remember asking Ekwunife to be my mentor; despite handling a tough and high-powered job, he generously gave his time to help me grow.

We met for an hour each month, such as our schedules allowed, and we grew closer to become friends. I visited his family homes in Ghana and the UK and was hosted by his lovely wife. They, too, visited our home in the UK. The main lesson for me here was that people will give more than you think they might, if you just ask.

Many leaders, irrespective of their race, are committed to growing talent and sharing wisdom, but I have observed that quite often aspiring leaders are too afraid to approach them and ask what they may think are the 'stupid' questions. However, it still pays to be judicious – the biggest turnoff for a leader who has little free time is to be asked for help and then having the junior be underprepared or unclear about what it is they seek when the meeting arrives.

Having a great boss helped me in delivering great results and achieving good annual ratings. Cristina Diezhandino, now chief marketing officer for Diageo globally, was the coolest person I had ever worked for – highly intelligent, hardworking, yet always calm and never flustered, she was influential for me.

It is important to have successful role models and to be associated with high-performing teams. I am proud to have earned my stripes under three members of the Diageo Africa exco team who went on to become global exco members. This is another aspect of making the right decisions in career advancement – alignment and association with those who are being recognised for doing good work.

All things must pass, as the saying goes. In early 2010, during the third year of my international assignment, I was already thinking about the fast-approaching date of March 2011, when I was scheduled to return to South Africa. What role would I be able to line up? Had I done well enough during my foreign assignment to get a promotion to what was then known as the Level 3 Executive Band? What about my wife and her career – what kind of job would she be able to find after she had sacrificed so much to move to the UK in support of my career?

Anyone who has spent time living overseas with a hard deadline for return will be able to empathise with the strange sense of unease and discomfort this can bring. It feels like being in a state of limbo for at least a year before the date arrives, and it's impossible to anticipate how things will go when you finally move back.

Most of the people I know who have worked on international sojourns have had to go through the process of lining up their next role back home, and it can be surprisingly difficult. It all comes down to timing, which means many returnees have to take on holding roles like special projects director or executive assistant in the CEO's office to keep busy until a more suitable permanent opportunity arises.

This is enough of a challenge, but typically there is also resettlement of family, the changing of schools for kids and other more mundane aspects of relocation to sort out. It can be a tough period emotionally, because while it's great to be coming back home, it often means leaving behind new networks of friends and colleagues you spent months or even years cultivating and having to start afresh.

Leaving behind the seductive convenience factor of living in developed countries like the US or the UK, where infrastructure functions smoothly, can also create a hard landing back home.

I was quite clear about what I was targeting when I left South Africa for a marketing role in the UK in 2008. My plan was to perform well enough in the role so that I could be promoted to Level 3 in the role of marketing and innovation director for South Africa or another market. I felt ready to run a business function as an executive director of a company. Wherever I landed, I wanted it to be in a senior leadership team or as part of an executive committee reporting to the CEO. From there, my career path, as I saw it, would be clear, with a definite conclusion. I thought I was someone who aspired to be a CEO, so it made sense for me to be a functional director as a next step in my career.

Before me, some of the people who had held regional marketing roles at Level 4 had gone on to become country marketing and innovation directors at Level 3, and for someone like me who loved benchmarking and planning, this all seemed like a natural and almost inevitable progression. Given what my family – and especially my wife – had sacrificed by following me to my role in the UK, I felt the progression *needed* to be inevitable.

I was blessed with options – some CEOs within Diageo offered me the opportunity to work in their markets as a marketing and innovation director, but my personal life had taken a turn through the loss of my father. I wanted to return home to spend quality time with my mother and reconnect with my friends and extended family after three years abroad.

I had set my sights on a marketing and innovation director role in South Africa, hence my decision to decline roles in other regions, but I was almost immediately disappointed – due to the high growth projection and complexity of the joint venture's demands on management, Diageo changed the South African role to a Level 2 job, instead of Level 3.

The incumbent marketing and innovation director would stay in his role as Diageo sought to take on South African Breweries (SAB). Their rationale was that they needed an experienced heavyweight director, which meant my promotion to a first-rotation functional director was delayed by a lack of experience.

Still believing I should move back home and not to another region, despite offers, I began thinking about what my Plan B could be. Fate intervened: I received a phone call from an executive search firm, who told me that Standard Bank was looking for a marketing director for its domestic business in South Africa. I jumped at the opportunity, though I battled a brief bout of impostor syndrome because of the size of the bank, its team and budget. Was I punching above my weight? I clearly had no experience with this type of business, and it sounded like a second-rotation marketing director role – requiring someone who was very familiar with the business and its dynamics.

No matter how confident you are in your own abilities, self-doubt never goes away. Just as those who engage in dangerous extreme sports claim they're still afraid but learn to cope with the fear, in business the equivalent is Richard Branson's famous quote: 'If somebody offers you an amazing opportunity but you are not sure you can do it, say yes – then learn how to do it later.'

Rationally, I thought, the recruiters must see something in me and my experience, and what did I have to lose? I could at least go meet the team and if the job didn't materialise, I would have learnt something from the process and possibly formed new relationships along the way. Even better, they offered to meet me in London for an interview, so the stars seemed to be aligning for me. The interviews went exceptionally well and I was asked to fly to Johannesburg for an interview with the CEO for South Africa, Sim Tshabalala, who would be my direct boss. Sim is now group CEO for Standard Bank. I was excited about working with him because, for the first time in my career, I was going to have a black boss – and the CEO of a major banking institution, no less!

He was a highly intelligent, soft-spoken, unassuming but strong leader. We immediately clicked at the interview and within a fortnight I received an offer for the marketing director role at one of Africa's largest banks. The remuneration package was so good that there was no point negotiating, so I accepted instantly.

The job ticked all the right boxes – it made my return to South Africa a grand re-entry into one of the highest-profile marketing jobs in the country, and, as far as I believed, completely validated my decision to step back into corporate from Nando's. It was also a show of strength to Diageo that their failure to appoint me to a higher-ranking director position had seen me land an even bigger role.

I was understandably happy, thinking my career path could not have turned out any better. I resigned from Diageo and began serving my three-month notice period. The company began recruiting for my successor while my new employer proudly announced my appointment and start date. My family began excitedly preparing for the return to South Africa.

Not for the first time in my life I surprised myself and everyone around me by changing my mind. I withdrew my resignation, deciding instead to stay with Diageo in the same role, doing the same job. No counteroffer was forthcoming. I risked my reputation and trustworthiness in South Africa by going back on the decision at the eleventh hour.

What really happened was that Nick Blazquez had been trying to arrange a time to speak with me, but his busy schedule had made this difficult because he had also recently assumed responsibility for parts of the European and Turkish business. By the time we got to meet, I was some way into serving my notice period, but my talk with him is what swayed me back to Diageo.

Nick was a global exco member for Diageo and was my boss's boss. I had previously told him about my career ambitions and asked him what it took to be a CEO. I had also sought counsel about what I needed to do to focus on my career development. He knew I cared about a CEO role and had taken time, at my request, to coach me in becoming a contender for a future CEO role.

I remember telling him that he had hired many CEOs during his time with the company, and was therefore most qualified to tell me whether I had what it took. I asked for an honest and frank appraisal, and the conversation gave me a kickstart because he was brutally honest. He told me I had a lot of work to do, which refocused my attention on the elements of leadership I needed to address.

Sometimes leaders can make the error of telling people what they think a junior would want to hear, rather than delivering a painful truth. This can, and has, set back many an aspirant business leader who has continued to operate under a false sense of achievement.

He asked me directly if I still had ambitions of becoming a CEO and, if so, how much did I care about it? This had always been my dream, so the answer was a simple yes, but he told me that, in his experience, banks never hire non-bankers as CEOs.

Secondly, even if they were ever to hire someone without a background in finance and banking, it would most likely take me much longer to build the necessary relationships, prove myself in the role and navigate the bank's internal politics. At Diageo, on the other hand, I had already done all the hard work and I was already on the cusp of landing a top job. I couldn't fault his logic. He told me I was already in the company's succession plans and that the business had been watching me for a while – and believed I was less than three years away from a CEO position. All it would take, he said, was to continue performing well.

If he was in charge when the time came – which he could never guarantee – I would land a CEO position. However, he said he believed in my capabilities so much that I would probably reach that level regardless of who was in charge at Diageo Africa.

What really did the trick for me was that Nick seemed to have my best interests at heart. He approached the conversation purely from a career management point of view, wanting to support me in reaching my goal and fulfilling my stated purpose.

'I can't put anything on paper because this is a conversation and not an offer, and things change, but you can trust me,' he said. That word – trust – was very reassuring to me. He sounded genuine, his body language corroborated what I was hearing and I believed I was talking with someone with integrity.

Most importantly, I was talking with someone who had hired many CEOs before, and here he was, telling me he would hire me as one. I couldn't see any reason why he would deceive me, and I knew this was a defining moment for me and my career. I decided then and there that I should not be sidetracked by the salary and title on offer at the bank and should stick with my trajectory at Diageo as a means of achieving what I thought was the ultimate prize.

Sometimes, in pursuit of short-term gratification and exciting prospects, we can lose sight of the bigger picture. It is important to know who your sponsors are, and to leverage them to grow to the top. Always try to deal with the decision maker, or someone who has direct access to the decision maker. Without this connection, it is difficult to have a sense of certainty about where you are headed.

Nick is a true gentleman and an absolute professional. He even offered to manage the fallout with the bank, since he knew some of the executives there after serving on boards in Africa with them. I chose to manage the discussion myself because I felt it was important to face up to my decision and be fully accountable. I also needed to maintain relationships, knowing that the world of business can be an awfully small place. Burning bridges was not something I could ever afford to do.

As for the bank, even if I became a CEO elsewhere, I would likely need funding at some point down the line and I had a pragmatic view of handling the situation. I arranged meetings and withdrew my acceptance. Fortunately, the bank was then engaged in a restructuring, which allowed them to manage external communication about my unexpected U-turn.

I also had to rebuild some relationships with Diageo – first with my line manager, who had already gone out to recruit a replacement and was about to extend an offer, and then with my colleagues, who were wondering what had happened. There was a suspicion that I had been induced to stay through some huge package, which was not the case.

After that, I had to deal with the speculation in the markets in which I had been serving, many of whom had already held farewells for me. There were many embarrassing moments, and the air of mystery remained for some time.

I was asked to stay in the UK for another year, as part of the discussions about my return to the company, because Diageo was also undergoing a restructuring exercise. There were no other big jobs going; I had been prepared and excited to return to South Africa, so it meant another period of adjustment for me and my family, but I fought to maintain focus. I knew that not everything would happen at my preferred time.

I had to wait and trust the system. Achieving great results would lessen the awkwardness of my backtracking, and I knew I was only as valuable as my latest set of results. Whatever Nick and Diageo may have thought of me, all businesses value consistent delivery.

My boss and I reconnected – she asked me to take on additional responsibility of managing digital marketing across Africa, and I also organised the inaugural Diageo Marketing Excellence Awards, sat on the panel of judges and was master of ceremonies at the event. Nick delivered opening remarks and handed out awards at the first event in Cape Town, and all regional CEOs were in attendance.

I had written out their lines and met them before the event to explain their roles and the flow of the evening, and this was a valuable opportunity to connect. Sometimes the world provides you with chances you have to take with both hands. Don't waste your opportunity to shine.

The awards were the perfect platform for rebuilding my reputation, but for the work I was doing as a regional marketer they also gave me the opportunity to cement relationships and showcase my talents. Though this seemed to come out of nowhere, I suspect my boss, being the strategic leader she is, had planned everything to happen just so. It worked like magic – this was the time for me to come out of the corner and show some leadership capabilities.

I was enjoying the best phase of my career, returning great results and working on my relationships across the African continent. My wife had also completed her MBA at Oxford and was working for a large pharmaceutical business in the UK. Diageo told me I was now ready for a promotion to Level 3 and would be a candidate for any roles that came up.

Not long after the business restructured, two Level 3 roles arose. One was as a marketing and innovation director in an African region, based in London. The other was as group portfolio head for whisky in South Africa. The hiring managers for both positions had identified me as a candidate and told me it was effectively my choice.

I had always aimed for a role as a marketing and innovation director, and this regional role was exciting because there were multiple countries involved – some of them new to Diageo. I would need to lead the marketing effort, working with the country CEOs and marketing teams, and for the first time I would be working for my mentor, whom I respected. He was the hiring manager, and it all looked simple to make the step to the promotion I had wanted.

It meant staying on in the UK for a total of seven years, but my family and I had begun to enjoy ourselves there and we felt settled. My wife's career was going well and a few more years of international experience would be beneficial, we agreed. Once more, all looked perfect.

The hiring manager in South Africa, who happened to be the country CEO, was not pleased with my decision and challenged it at the executive meeting where talent was discussed. He knew me well and had identified me as the leader who could step up the growth of the whisky business, which was facing increasingly stiff competition in South Africa, especially in the standard and value market segments.

From a general manager point of view the whisky role was exciting, but in my mind it was less challenging to be dealing with a smaller portfolio. I was extremely conscious of my embarrassment at already turning down the bank's offer and I was set on managing public perception of my decisions, even if the South African role was still a promotion to Level 3.

I rejected the South African offer. This did not go down well back home, with the local business reminding me that I was originally sponsored to go the UK as part of succession plans from a local talent pool. I was effectively told I should come home and serve. This required treading carefully: the South African CEO was a good friend, and had been an incredible mentor who had helped me through many career decisions. I was lucky to have had Gerald Mahinda in my life. But this was an intractable situation – either way, I would be reneging on a decision yet again.

Nick, as a line manager to both hiring managers who wanted me, was asked to intervene and find a solution. He asked both parties to make a final attempt at resolving the dispute themselves, and to then tell me where I should be deployed. This, at least, would absolve me of choosing sides. But they still disagreed, and Nick was forced to make a judgement call.

Again, Nick explained his thought processes, concluding that I should go back to South Africa and take the whisky job. He told me it may not have made sense at the time, but that it was best for the business. The whisky business in South Africa carried the performance of the region he led, because of its scale and high margins, so he needed a leader he could trust to grow the business and leverage it to fund business development in Africa. Knowing me, he thought I was best for the role.

While I stabilised the whisky business, the CEO could be freed to focus on the beer business, which faced its own challenges due to complex joint venture structures and an aggressive competitor. In closing, he told me it was a favour he was asking that he would not forget, bearing in mind that he knew my CEO ambitions.

I was confused: if I was not being offered a functional director role, I would not be gaining the type of experience I needed in South Africa to be eligible for a promotion to CEO within the three years he had spoken of the first time we met. Was this not actually slowing me down? I would still need to gain experience as a functional director before becoming eligible. Nick told me he was aware of this, but that career advancement was not always linear. I reluctantly agreed to return to South Africa, with the added complication of living in Johannesburg but working in Cape Town, commuting every Monday and Friday.

The whisky role turned out to provide some incredible achievements, like the Keep Walking South Africa campaign for the iconic Johnnie Walker brand, relaunching J&B and expanding the reach of the Bells brand. We also strategised for the relaunch of the value offering in the stable, and I think my team from that time probably still ranks as the best and most balanced I have worked with.

Talented, high-energy individuals spanning races and genders, at 60 per cent female and 50 per cent black, they were passionate and knowledgeable. I really like working with a great team – people who push my thinking but also respect my input and leadership. We had fun, we created magic and smashed our targets.

My boss, Gavin Krenski, who did not play a high-profile role in the recruitment process, was simply outstanding – no politics, no ego, just focused on team unity and delivering great results. I worked well with him and treated him with the utmost respect. He remains one of the most brilliant marketing minds in the business, and an amazing leader. I remember the many sessions we had in his house in Claremont, where he generously hosted the team. We achieved much in a very short space of time.

Just 18 months later I answered a phone call from Nick, who surprised me by telling me that he'd recommended me for a role as managing director and CEO for Uganda Breweries Limited (UBL) and that I needed to prepare to fly to Nairobi the following week for an interview with the hiring manager.

This was one of the most exciting phone calls I have ever received. I went for that interview and withstood a proper grilling for two hours, but a week later I was offered my dream job. In September of 2013, at the age of 37, I started in my role as CEO of UBL, with my own board, chairman, two manufacturing plants and some eight hundred employees. I had arrived, and Nick had stayed true to his word. Again, I had learnt to slow down to move faster.

5

A GIANT LEAP IN UGANDA

My three years spent in Uganda as CEO of UBL were a dream come true and the experience of running the business played a formative role in the executive leader I have become today.

This was the opportunity for me to prove to Diageo that they'd made the right decision. I was well acquainted with the spirits market, but beer as a business was relatively new to me and I knew there would be a steep learning curve. There was another, more daunting, prospect – I would also have to deal with a company board for the first time. I'd never even reported directly to a CEO before.

I had six weeks to prepare my family for leaving and deal with the logistics of relocating to Kampala. I experienced a lot of tension but found it useful for growing into a top role. If you're overconfident, you will not make enough of an effort to succeed. I felt excited to be learning and growing, and in my typical style I wanted to be as prepared as possible.

I set about identifying gaps in my experience and knowledge I would need to address before hitting the ground in Kampala. I also needed to find support to help me address the gaps. I was fortunate to have an executive coach in Charles Mead, based in the UK. He knew my ambition and he had already prepared me for the job interviews and the role. We discussed all aspects of the challenge to come, and since he'd also coached my future boss, this was very useful in preparing me holistically for what was to come.

Charles and I identified three key areas where I needed support: first, a general understanding of the issues in the Ugandan business, which had been losing market share and experiencing declining profitability for years. I was clear about my task at UBL – a turnaround of a business that was on the ropes, despite apparently competent leadership.

The second personal hurdle was overcoming a lack of experience as a CEO. I had little previous experience in finance and leveraging a balance sheet, which meant I was going to be reliant on UBL's CFO, who'd also had ambitions for the CEO role before I was appointed. Managing our personal relationship in the aftermath of a contest for the top role was going to be crucial to getting the support I needed in getting to grips with the company's financials.

The last major task before I landed in the country was getting up to speed on supply chain management. A company like UBL spends a lot of money insourcing products for the brewery, like tanks, boilers and brewing line equipment, and I had to learn about efficiencies, warehousing, distribution, imports, spare parts and inventory management, among many other intricacies that would give me the full picture of the business.

In short, I had to learn a new language. Coming from a commercial background, there was a lot to learn. I love strategy, but operational issues were not my strong point.

Once we had outlined my areas for improvement and made plans to address them, my next order of business was to consider my network within Uganda. I needed friends to soften the landing, and I needed help navigating all the stakeholders, cultural considerations and politics of a new country.

All of these considerations were inputs for my 100-day plan designed to prevent me from landing 'cold', which meant a very busy six weeks. I still needed to close off my role at Diageo in South Africa and ensure a smooth handover to my successor.

I contacted some key players like Gerald Mahinda, who had previously held the position of EABL CEO and who helped me understand the Ugandan business's legacy issues. Peter Ndegwa, a former CFO of EABL, had recently been appointed as CEO for Diageo in Ghana and similarly served as a coach during my transition as I learnt from him how to adapt to the role and the politics among functional directors.

I also received help from the former CFO of Brandhouse Beverages, Martin Kromat, to whom I posed one simple question: 'I'm a newly appointed CEO. How does a person like me manage a person like you?' Brandhouse was a fascinating company that existed for only a decade, from 2004 to 2014, as a joint venture between Diageo, Heineken and Namibia Breweries. By joining forces, these three companies could build scale in their distribution and logistics operations to compete effectively with very dominant SAB brands.

Being typically direct, Martin gave an energising and impactful answer, and the conversation provided me with some tools for dealing with the CFO so that I didn't appear all at sea when it came to debt ratios, interest cover, cash flow, provisions and so on.

I was generally very direct in whatever I was trying to find out and found fellow leaders very willing to contribute. I received many offers for ongoing remote support once I started in Uganda, which was brilliant. The lesson I was learning was that sometimes you need benchmarks and role models to help you get to where you need to be.

For supply chain management I contacted a former Brandhouse supply chain director, Henk van Klompenburg, and exposed my vulnerability by asking him how a brewery worked. Henk was kind enough to explain in depth all the theory around efficiencies and took me to the Brandhouse brewery in Sedibeng, Gauteng, which I hadn't visited before.

We walked the facility for me to appreciate the art of making beer: the strengths and weaknesses of our competition, taxation, raw material sourcing and more. Most importantly, he told me what to look for if my supply chain managers were not doing a good job. This allowed me to land in Uganda with a greater amount of confidence. I had constructed a cheat sheet for managing my directors.

Gerald Mahinda supplied me with a piece of advice which was to become invaluable to me. He told me to visit the brewery at unusual times to observe the goings-on for myself. His advice was to take photos and to present them as visual evidence if I found anything out of order. Visual records never lie, as he said.

Finally, I called on Brenda Mbathi, corporate relations director for EABL, and Joe Heshu, who was corporate affairs director for British

American Tobacco at the time. Joe proved to be very useful to me, having worked with the Department of International Relations. He introduced me to the head of the South African mission in Uganda and, ultimately, the South African ambassador to Uganda.

When I arrived, because I'd already met these people through sharing emails, one of the first things I did was to present myself and my CFO, Alvin Mbugua, to the ambassador at his office. We developed a great relationship with the late Jon Qwelane, who showed us around and introduced us to key political figures. Within weeks of arriving I felt I'd had all the right interactions with key government officials in Uganda.

Brenda is Kenyan but had spent much time working in Uganda and understood the political landscape well. I was amazed by how generous people were, which eased the settling-in process immensely.

I began on 1 September 2013 and tested my 100-day plan in the real world. My line manager, EABL CEO Charles Ireland, laid out his expectations for the business and the direction we needed to take. This was a stiff challenge, since three years is not a lot of time to turn a business around, but I knew that if I could get it right it would serve as a stepping stone to bigger things. I had already jumped ahead to a role usually offered to a second-rotation CEO, so I was excited about what was in store if I could excel in the Ugandan role.

I began to execute at pace, with my fixed-term contract always at the back of my mind. I was already developing plans to return to South Africa and step into a Level 2 CEO role with Diageo once I was done in Uganda, so I put myself under pressure to show my worth.

Shortly after my arrival I attended a Johnnie Walker Symphony in Blue event hosted by the then-chairman of the Absa business in Uganda, Swithin Munyantwali, now Absa Group non-executive director and a top global lawyer. This was the ultimate event in the Johnnie Walker brand's calendar, and was only the second of its type to be held in Uganda. It really got me thinking. The event brought in whisky experts from around the world and about thirty of the who's who in Uganda attended. I decided to host my own whisky tasting and experience event, and invite all my business counterparts for a meet-and-greet.

But I wanted to take this event to the next level.

The invitations were pitched as the new CEO of UBL wanting to introduce himself, and we called on all the captains of industry, distributors, suppliers and government. The event was hosted in the garden of my newly rented house and limited to 40 couples. I made sure this was the event everyone wanted to be at, and it became a trend for CEOs and entrepreneurs to host these events privately.

The media talked about this event for months and it did wonders for my profile, but there was another unexpected upside – we sold an enormous quantity of Johnnie Walker Blue Label at a good margin and the events were hugely profitable. At one event hosted by one of Uganda's wealthiest people, we shifted about eight hundred bottles of Johnnie Walker Blue Label, which was quite possibly a world record for a private event.

That event put me and UBL on the map instantly. It also led to Johnnie Walker Blue Label becoming the de facto gifting option for the wealthy and the opening of the JWBL Experience Store in the Sheraton Hotel in Kampala – one of only a few in the world at that time.

Back at UBL, one of the things Charles Mead had advised me to do was to quickly assess my team and decide who I wanted to work with. I needed people who would be loyal to my vision and capable of executing what I wanted done. When I arrived, the executive team was full of expatriate executives, mostly male. By the time I left, the team was 50 per cent female and comprised mostly Ugandans. I replaced more than half the executives, reduced and consolidated roles, and was ultimately succeeded by a Ugandan.

Even better, the Ugandan CEO was then succeeded by my CFO, Alvin, whom I had sponsored for the CEO role in future and whose readiness I actively drove. I am immensely proud of Alvin, who has since been promoted to lead the Diageo business in Central America and the Caribbean. I forced him to take on more operational tasks to realise his potential, after which he was identified as a head of sales over in Kenya before being sent back to Uganda as CEO.

I assembled a new team, which has remained at the core of UBL's leadership since my departure. I headhunted Ademola Adeoye as sales director from Nigeria. For me, the first stage of the turnaround had to be getting the right people into those roles. The common denominator was that I chose youthful and energetic executives who wanted to prove to themselves and the company that they could deliver.

The other important factor was how the executive team complemented each other – healthy debate, good tension and vibrant team dynamics were important for a successful turnaround. I don't really care about roles per se – what I really want is someone who is commercially minded. Business must drive sustainability and contribute to society, but to do that it must be commercially successful, so what can you do to enable that?

I selected a young team with hunger to make things happen, and that was instrumental in the turnaround, but my sales background also drew my attention to our salespeople – many of whom were frankly glorified order takers and administrators. Exacerbating the lack of real sales skills was a requirement that they all report to Kampala regularly. This meant they were travelling more than they were facing customers.

I wanted the sales team to use technology to allow them to stay in their territories for longer. We also needed to sort out some known issues with internal controls and compliance breaches. I was alarmed by the lack of basic capabilities in selling, so one of my first tasks was to set up competency tests for our sales team. Working with one of the leading global consulting houses on our route to the customer, we redefined our sales strategy and reach, as well as the tools we wanted for equipping the team. Then we defined role profiles against our existing team members.

We called in an agency to assess the team and more than half failed. We had to let them go. The market in Uganda didn't provide many ready-made salespeople, so we brought in fresh graduates from local universities and trained them. It was a huge discontinuity risk, but our sales improved by double digits because the youngsters had so much energy and were innovative. Even the remaining older salespeople raised their games and really started to deliver.

Next up was tackling the fraud problem I had been warned about. Everyone who had worked at UBL was concerned about the lack of governance, but my way of dealing with it was to clearly and transparently reward delivery and performance while punishing non-performance. Without experience, youngsters found themselves being promoted and even seconded abroad to other Diageo divisions.

Suddenly, from being a relative backwater, Uganda boasted the largest number of nationals working abroad within Diageo. We sent 11 Ugandans elsewhere and they continued to be ambassadors for UBL. This was a volte-face from the previous situation of UBL being full of expats, and the profile of UBL within Diageo began to rise.

Why would I send my most skilled performers away? My view was that, if I sent my best employees out of the market, it would not only create room for more talent to filter through, but it would also serve as inspiration for those lower down. The relationship between performance and reward needed to be obvious.

Slowly, UBL became more competitive. There were consequences – both positive and negative – for delivery, and the discrimination was defendable. Those who didn't perform either left or were asked to leave. Sometimes business is about just getting the basics right.

My original mandate was to turn around a progressive loss of market share over eight years that threatened the sustainability of the business. Starting from the top, we needed a high-performance culture: a culture of ownership, a culture of delivery, a culture of winning. When I arrived, the team was feeling beaten by strong beer competitors and heads were down. Yet, the behaviour of most employees was astonishing because they still behaved like they were market leaders. Nothing in their pay packages, benefits, increases or the way of doing business had changed. There were no consequences for losing.

I had to shock the system, which suffered from a legacy of the business's origins as a state-owned enterprise where the attitude was that you could come to work, park and collect a salary. Just like with those lower down who were dragging their feet, I needed to let go of my direct reports who were not getting their hands dirty.

Turning my attention to external factors, I focused on stakeholder management. I was inspired by the innovative approach brought into Diageo by global CEO Ivan Menezes, who assumed the top job in July 2013 – just before I took over at UBL. Ivan brought a new energy to the group, and he had a clear 10-point plan for where Diageo's focus should be. One of these points was to invest, grow and innovate within our portfolio. We needed to show 15 per cent of net revenue from products that were five years old or younger, to encourage reinvention. By the end of a rolling five-year period, this would mean substantial portfolio optimisation and innovation, which kept us thinking about how consumer habits and needs were changing.

I love innovation and have endured sleepless nights worrying about being able to offer our customers what they want. Once products reach a level of parity in how they deliver, that is where people can really start making choices – that's where the game is.

The beauty of Diageo globally was that there was a lot of innovation in packaging, product design and cost cutting. Without access to the research and design resources of some of the largest global brands, I had to take some pointers from what they had come up with.

Over 60 per cent of the revenue came from three local brands – Bell Lager, Senator Trademark and Uganda Waragi gin, all locally produced. This was exciting because Uganda Waragi was not one of the global priority brands that Diageo controlled centrally to ensure consistent and careful branding, so we could improvise or take ideas from elsewhere and localise with pride. With brands that were only present in Uganda, I had the freedom to make the changes I wanted.

Uganda Waragi had scale in Uganda and was much loved, but we could still innovate. We didn't have to work with the central innovation resource. We were allowed to localise. With Smirnoff, we were allowed to make a local flavour because they knew flavours work well. We had carte blanche with ideas for Waragi.

This was an enticing prospect. Uganda's young demographic profile led to the market being quite experimental, so our first move was to take a local gin (though, going by its taste, it is a gin in name only) called

Uganda Waragi and transform its bottle, which had already been copied by all other gin producers. I wanted to create a premium-looking, sleek bottle. The example set by Smirnoff was that a significant improvement in performance can be achieved through a simple change in packaging.

We needed the best bottle in the market, and to find a way to change it while reducing costs. This was achievable without excessive spend on tooling and I felt the outcome was amazing. Next, we jumped onto the global trend towards flavours and experimented with the launch of coffee, coconut and other flavours of Uganda Waragi, working with a global flavour house.

We were able to add these flavours, benefitting from economies of scale within Diageo, which was a huge advantage for us. Local waragi makers could not do the same. Coconut waragi was an instant hit and it improved our margins – we even introduced it in sachets that were so popular we couldn't match demand. We found an affordable sachet-making machine in India and brought it to Uganda at a decent price. Our output was raised and so was our profitability.

My boss, Charles Ireland, was supportive when we motivated for capital expenditure. To him, while governance and ethics were important, output and numbers were what mattered. If our numbers were good, he didn't interfere. We met weekly for me to brief him, but generally I was left to do my job.

I also felt supported by our board chairman, Dr Alan Shonubi, who was keen to see our brands grow and thrive. While he would hold me and my team to account, he was also extremely supportive of our decisions and helped us navigate a complex market. Without his support and counsel, our innovations would not have worked.

Uganda Waragi was a huge success, reviving a spirits business that had been under pressure. UBL's 30-year-old spirit line had effectively been replaced.

Dr Shonubi was passionate about Bell Lager, but the brand was tired. The label was of poor quality and the product was not performing. A previous attempt at improving profitability had seen a change in the bottle and the recipe, which was a terrible mistake. I am big on quality, so finding the product in store with skew labels was just a bad look for Bell, as far as I was concerned. People buy with their eyes. The problem was that Uganda was a returnable bottle market, so any additional change to the bottle meant writing off an enormous quantity of expensive bottle stock.

Inspired by Guinness, we transformed Bell's label. Our creative team worked magic with the new label – it turned out beautifully. We also fixed some quality and leakage issues in the bottling, and the brand started to grow again.

Senator was another UBL beer that was flagging. I decided to take a very bold step. Senator came in two variants – the regular version at 5.5 per cent ABV and a stronger version with more alcohol content – but the brand was suffering from reputational issues of being watery-tasting, sugary and weak.

We launched Senator Stout, the first and only locally produced stout in Uganda. The hurdle we had to overcome was operating within Diageo and getting permission to launch what was perceived to be a competitor to Guinness. Undercutting Guinness was frowned upon, but after jumping through many hoops within the company we were able to introduce it as a reimagined brand. Senator Stout was highly profitable because it targeted a whole new market segment that Guinness was unable to reach. It was a daring move that pushed the envelope, but it worked because I was willing to ask the uncomfortable questions.

My most satisfying and daring innovation at UBL, however, was the launch of Ngule beer. Early during my contract in Uganda, I found in our archive a proposal from the Buganda Kingdom, the largest nation within Uganda, which constitutes nearly half of the population. Majestic Brands – the investment arm of the Buganda Kingdom – had been looking at licensing their name and working with companies to monetise products that would provide them with royalty revenue. The proposal hadn't been taken up because of UBL's concerns about linkages to government institutions, and the Kingdom had subsequently contracted a competitor to produce Crown lager. This attempt failed and the product was discontinued.

When I stumbled upon the proposal, I started thinking about UBL's failure to dominate the value sector of the beer market, which was dominated by our competitors but offered 50 per cent of the total market's volume.

While UBL led in other segments of the beer market, we were struggling to compete at the lower-priced end. I thought, if Senator had reputation issues, why didn't we just launch a completely new brand with no baggage? While it would add to complexity in the market and came with challenges, partnering with the Buganda king would mean the king championing the brand to offset the cost of marketing.

At the same time, the proposal came with a great story behind it – the Kingdom wanted to use royalties from the beer to fund community centres and clinics, and improve education for its people. I decided we needed to meet with the king and prime minister, and develop the beer in accordance with the king's wishes – what it should taste like, the colour scheme, the ABV content, price point. At every step we sought consultation.

We also ensured that all ingredients would be authentic, including starches grown only in that part of Uganda. It was a good-news story all round because local farmers would also benefit from the success of the beer.

The difficulty lay in obtaining approval to do business with a government institution, which was discouraged at Diageo. We did get approval and created history for the African continent. Ngule was launched, and moved from zero market share to 7 per cent in the first six months.

We ran out of stock, with the king's staff encouraging Buganda people to switch brands. Our competitors didn't see it coming and couldn't stop it. Innovation, innovation, innovation – things must not stand still and speed to market counts, just as Mike Joubert had told me at Diageo in Cape Town all those years ago.

Despite success stories like these, which remain some of the best in my career, naturally I could not escape failures. As so many leaders have said before, we need to recognise that we will sometimes fail, but what matters is how you manage yourself during the crisis and bounce back to restore confidence.

My advice is to be realistic and open to the fact that not everything will go your way. There will be results and events that disappoint you, your bosses and your workmates. It is important to recognise when to give up and move on. Sometimes failure is staring you in the face and it's not worth wasting further time and resources on trying to save face.

If you register more successes than failures, you will be fine – especially if, as with Diageo, there is a common understanding that innovation will sometimes work and sometimes fall flat. Just capture the learnings and bounce back.

One notable failure during my time in Uganda was the attempt to launch a ready-to-drink (RTD) product for Uganda Waragi. Diageo had scored many successes globally with RTD products and in South Africa I had led the RTD portfolio, so I thought we could easily replicate it in Uganda. I thought it would be as simple as asking Ugandans what the most popular flavours to incorporate would be.

From market research we settled on ginger as the runaway favourite and approached a flavour house to mix it up for us. The consumer testing went well and we aimed to launch the product during the peak December period. The brewery was busy at that time, but we found a gap over at EABL in Kenya and had to order the whole production run to be ready for the launch. Our forecasts demanded a large amount of stock.

We rushed and skipped some crucial steps, including consumer testing of the first batch to be produced at scale. The product didn't taste like the prototype, and they didn't pick it up at EABL because it was new to the market and was not going to be distributed in Kenya. We brought in truckloads of the new product, and it was undrinkable. The internal and external launches were a flop and we had to write off the entire stock.

What saved the day was being able to reuse the bottles with new labels. I had previously learned a valuable lesson in never investing in bespoke product packaging until it's proven, so although the lost liquid cost us a fair amount and was hugely embarrassing, everything else was reusable.

That misstep destroyed the potential for Uganda Waragi to produce an

RTD product for a few years to come. We had primed the launch and I had pushed for it to happen because I wanted to execute at speed before our competitors could bring out their own offerings. A hallmark of my leadership style is speed, which saves money and can beat competition, but it was a mistake to cut corners. I have since learnt that this kind of overconfidence is a common ailment among CEOs.

It is wise to surround yourself with an executive team that pushes back when other directors are not comfortable, but our previous successes in innovation had made us all simply too bullish to be measured enough in our approach to this product. It was humbling and necessary, but we took the punches – there is no success without setbacks.

Another failure during my leadership of UBL was when we wanted to champion the relaunch of Bell Lager – I decided we needed to shout from the rooftops about rejuvenating our flagship beer, which was highly profitable and had so much going for it. It was made from local raw materials, with more than 15 000 farmers producing sorghum to brew the beer. It was a great story in terms of value chain benefits.

What could be a better announcement than bringing a globally renowned hip hop star to Uganda? No beer brand had ever been able to land a coup like that – I believed we would be punching above our weight in an economy under pressure. Only the telecoms giants like Airtel and MTN had been able to splash such money to attract international performing artists.

After seemingly endless negotiations and lots of money spent, we signed a deal to bring Neo to Uganda. It was a big deal – people could hardly believe it. True to my maverick approach I went a step further and declared it should be a no-ticket event, by invitation only. We booked a venue to hold 10 000 people and the advertising stated that only consumers of Bell could be rewarded with a ticket in a lucky draw system.

Our plan was to issue 2 000 tickets per week. Bell buyers could send a unique code from under the bottle top via SMS to stand a chance of being randomly selected. But it didn't go to plan. There was fraud reported in the collection of tickets, to the extent that we had at best issued 20 per cent of the tickets with one week to go before the concert.

It seemed like a great idea to drive market share and popularity, but it all went horribly wrong. There was a backlash of consumer anger and activism about their rights to attend even as non-Bell drinkers, exposing weaknesses in the campaign. This type of campaign had been successful previously in South Africa and I'm nothing if not good at modifying ideas for markets, but I had to concede defeat and we released the tickets for sale in the final week.

We may not have generated the sales the campaign was designed to create, but the concert was sold out and it was a spectacle. It worked to reveal the new brand in fantastic fashion and was talked about for a long time afterwards. I learnt that when you lead people you need to avoid stepping on their toes – I wanted to add value, but I also needed to be wary of stifling our strategy and marketing directors to ensure they could also add value.

One major contributor to a successful term for me in Uganda was that my leadership style differed markedly from that of previous CEOs. I was intent on establishing a connection with employees on the ground and was very particular about being accessible to everyone.

I'm fascinated by people and curious about what drives them. I want to know what makes them go the extra mile and what I can do to support their performance. This is visible servant leadership, but it came as a surprise to employees at UBL.

I had been astonished to find I had a huge office waiting for me, with a secondary office for my personal assistant as gatekeeper. The route to my office also ensured I went unseen by all other employees. I was even served food, which was ordered externally and delivered to my office, while the rest of the staff ate at our canteen.

This went against the global trend towards transparency and the demystification of leadership. Since I generate energy from being around other people, I made some immediate changes. I told my PA I would be eating in the canteen twice a week. She was horrified and warned me against the food there, but I said, if it's good enough for them, it is good enough for me.

Truck drivers, cleaners, administration clerks – everyone was taken aback when I'd sit at their tables and talk freely. I gained a lot of insight into what was really happening in the company – things my supply chain director wouldn't disclose. I would also – on the advice I was given – visit the brewery unannounced, at times, like at 3 a.m. on a Saturday.

The employees working such shifts or driving trucks across Uganda overnight on dangerous roads are the unsung heroes of the business and I needed to acknowledge them. Sometimes I'd arrive with pizzas and soft drinks, and we'd shoot the breeze. To my surprise, I was almost always asked to pose for photos – such was the novelty of a CEO taking an interest in their functions.

I decided we needed to renovate the UBL offices to create an open-plan work environment, which would destroy the legacy of architecturally enforced hierarchy. Without spending an inordinate amount on the refurbishment we broke down interior walls, put up glass walls to increase both transparency and natural light, got rid of my offices and made better use of the space. I had a meeting room instead, and anyone was able to walk right up to my desk to talk to me.

The revamp of the canteen was a particular highlight because we transformed it into a multipurpose space that could be used for functions and product launches. We also installed a rooftop bar with an amazing view of Lake Victoria, kitted out by professional decorators. This provided another boost to employee morale because it demonstrated that we cared about them.

As a CEO, you come to understand quickly that your job is not from 9 a.m. to 5 p.m. – if your products are being used all day, every day, there is no downtime and you are always on standby. I was thankful to have married a doctor, for whom this kind of work ethic was second nature, so she was very understanding if I'd leave the dinner table to conduct a trade visit at a local tavern or pop in at the brewery for a check-up.

I once read a quote that an office is a dangerous place from which to run a business, and I agree fully. If the people buying your products are in spaza shops in unsophisticated circumstances, you need to appreciate your value chain and be streetwise in connecting with customers. A lot of executives I knew had become more disconnected the higher they rose in the ranks within corporates, but the person I wanted to connect with was the hardworking barlady who was serving my customers. If I saw my competitor's bottles on the bar counter or found that one of our fridges hadn't been working for two weeks, or that there were no good pricing promotions driving sales, these were the clues I needed to make changes at our weekly exco meetings.

Hilariously, my Friday trade visits were to disturb my direct reports, who feared what I might be seeing on my travels. My PA, Dorcus Kanyago, and my driver were the only people who knew my planned route, and they were often pressed for tip-offs because sales teams are notorious for dressing the bride for trade visits. Eventually, technology was my undoing, with an exco WhatsApp group betraying the movements of my vehicle, whose appearance – a cream-coloured Land Rover – was unusual enough to spot from a mile off.

Another upside of this cat-and-mouse trade visit game was that I used to sometimes jump into our sales representatives' vehicles to ride along, which led to an improvement in the maintenance and safety regime for our fleet.

A cornerstone of my leadership style was conducting regular town-hall meetings with employees, where we'd have an opportunity to engage and ask questions. I wanted to celebrate performance and milestones, but also field the uncomfortable questions. These events became quite theatrical because we made an effort to bring everyone together in seeing their part in our vision. When we talked about numbers and targets, people could see their roles and contributions.

When UBL employees were given bonuses for performance and saw how their work was being rewarded, the baseline was ratcheted up another notch to reinforce the performance culture. Our people were receiving the highest bonuses in the industry. Motivation was everywhere.

Our net promoter score kept improving, to the point where we placed in the top 20 globally and first in Africa. Employees were energised, excited and working hard, owning their roles in the business. This was not a qualitative perception – our numbers didn't lie. We were growing profits in double digits, faster than our top-line growth.

We eliminated waste and the business became innovative, seeking solutions and alternatives. I began to see evidence of a lesson I'd learnt years before: if you want to succeed in a corporate, your role moves beyond your day job. Your job description is the minimum of what you do. To grow, you need to demonstrate your true value to the organisation.

If you're a marketing manager, are you involved in the graduate programme and are you championing the company's charitable initiatives? Are you getting involved in the corporate culture change project? Are you driving transformation and the empowerment of women? What else are you doing to change the organisation?

I believe 80 per cent of any employee's time should be spent on driving business results, with 20 per cent spent on building the organisation. The organisation is forever evolving and needs all of us to work outside our day jobs to build it. Organisations, by extension, help build the country. As you become more senior, building the business becomes more closely aligned with building the organisation. Functional leaders need to bring it all together in thought leadership – external stakeholders, government, regulators, shareholders, the board and employees.

My involvement in the Uganda Manufacturers' Association, which is a presidential economic advisory group, was significant because every country needs public–private partnerships to drive growth. I came to understand how important a strategic corporate relations department is. Real growth requires more than lobbying – it involves planning with government to drive GDP growth, from which businesses benefit.

My relationship with Ambassador Qwelane led to a few engagements, such as being asked to act as master of ceremonies for the Nelson Mandela memorial held in Kampala, which allowed me to network with the president and prime minister of Uganda, while forging other relationships that I could leverage for all aspects of our business: distribution, supply, finance and so on. Never waste a good opportunity to open more doors.

My final highlight from my time in Uganda, however, relates internally to Diageo. Before my term at UBL, the business suffered from a low profile as a small market with waning relevance and declining margins selling only local brands. Diageo was considering divesting as the business declined in profitability.

Great work attracts recognition. On arrival I was told the president of Diageo Africa had not been to Uganda in eight years, despite visiting Ethiopia and Tanzania to inspect brewery investments. During my three years at UBL he visited three times, given the news of our jumps in profitability, and then the coup de grâce came when the Diageo global CEO Ivan Menezes was due to visit Uganda on holiday.

What a fortuitous occasion – here was the global CEO of a business operating in more than 130 countries, with 80 of them strong enough to require regular visits that would clog up his diary for 18 months if he saw even one per week, coming to Uganda for the first time. It was not an opportunity to miss.

Uganda's scenic beauty and famous gorillas had helped lure him, but it was still a momentous event and we knew we had to make the most of it. Ivan was kind enough to change his plans to arrive in Uganda a day before his family so that he could visit the business. While we could control the itinerary and route while he was with us, we had no idea where he would be headed on the following four days while he was on holiday, so preparation of all possible trade outlets was intense.

We had to get our house in order, making sure all our brands were well located. This was an opportunity to be featured in his weekly newsletter, which would make UBL – in Diageo terms – world-famous.

Ironically, it so happened that the global CEO of SABMiller, our competitor, was also coming to Uganda in the week before Ivan's arrival. What were the odds? We were in a two-horse race to ensure good product placement and visibility of promotional posters.

The British embassy in Uganda agreed to host a reception for Ivan, and we again leveraged our connections to show that the Uganda business was taken seriously, setting up a meeting with the Ugandan president and prime minister.

Having admired Ivan's leadership from a distance for some time, particularly his humble, easy-going approach, I was personally extremely excited by the opportunity. I felt like we had a connection that went back to our upbringings in ordinary circumstances – his in India and mine in Gazankulu.

Ivan may have been open and personable, but he was also tough, demanding and smart. He was thrilled to see the reality of what was happening in Uganda, even as it was obvious that we faced stiff competition in our markets. We tried to squeeze in as many trade visits as possible and the quality of conversation was like friends getting together over a drink. It brought home to me that business really is all about connecting with people.

I aspire to be a leader like Ivan in terms of that attitude. The Ugandan president's office called to say he had been delayed during a trip to China and wanted to reschedule a visit during Ivan's holiday time, so he agreed to fly back to Kampala for the meeting. The problem was that I was supposed to be back in South Africa over the Easter weekend on that date. I would typically head back home over long weekends to get a break from work, and my wife and two sons were already in South Africa in anticipation of me wrapping up the final phase of my assignment in Uganda.

Ivan was insistent that I needed to be with my family, since our youngest son had just been born. Since this wasn't planned for, we also wouldn't have the use of arranged transport and security, but Ivan told me he would use my car – adjusting to the situation in a flexible way. What a mindful, pragmatic leader.

The Diageo president of Africa had enough confidence in me to allow me to host Ivan with Charles Ireland, and Charles himself stayed largely in the background while we showed Ivan around. The level of trust placed in me was remarkable. I helped Ivan prepare his speech for the reception and all went off smoothly until time came to take Ivan back to the airport. There had been a misunderstanding about his schedule – he had another 12 hours to kill, and wanted to go back out to trade outlets late on a Friday night!

We had nothing planned, but the time difference from the United States was such that Ivan was feeling energetic and said he'd had enough of the high-end trade outlets. He wanted to see where low-income consumers bought and drank our products. Unscheduled and unplanned, we hit the streets of Kampala's downmarket areas, jumping muddy potholes and mixing with the locals. I'd never seen Ivan so alive.

Ultimately, I would come to be offered a promotion greater than I'd even hoped for, thanks to my successful stint in Uganda, and such memories will stay with me for the rest of my life. Business can be reduced to simplicity: Deliver a better customer experience, drive revenue, inspire your staff and decrease costs. It's the personal connections along the way that are essential.

6

THE RED REVOLUTION

I am tremendously proud of my achievements during my three years at Vodacom. My track record running the business unit that accounted for 70 per cent of the group's revenue in South Africa validated my approach as a business leader after 15 years with Diageo.

I had been well supported by Diageo and was promoted after my time in Uganda, to return home as CEO for Diageo South Africa – which was at least three times bigger than the company's presence in Uganda – and to report directly to the president of Diageo Africa, a global exco member reporting to Ivan Menezes. But my reason for moving was more about Vodacom than Diageo. I was not actively looking for other opportunities, but when a recruitment agency contacted me I was intrigued by their pitch.

Not for the first time in my career I seemed an unlikely candidate, but the recruiters told me that Vodafone – the international holding company of Vodacom – had rejigged its recruitment strategy to target executives from consumer goods companies to run their consumer business units. This approach, credited to Vodafone's regional CEO for Africa, the Middle East, Asia and the Pacific, Serpil Timuray, resonated with me. I was unsurprised to learn that Serpil had come from Danone via P&G. Her success as CEO of Danone in Turkey had led to an offer from Vodafone, which in turn led to a larger regional role, inspiring a new approach to executive recruitment at Vodafone.

Vodacom's decision to blend external candidates with those who had 'grown up' within the group, like CEO Shameel Joosub, was commendable. There was a general feeling that the business needed fresh, independent ideas. While some candidates had grown towards the position from within the company, I had been approached because

I would not be entrenched in the same way of thinking and would have no blind spots to potential revenue streams.

Vodacom is one of the biggest businesses in South Africa in terms of success and profitability, and I was also aware of Vodacom's strong brand as an employer of choice. I had always nurtured a clear vision of ascending to the role of CEO of a JSE-listed business, so I saw Vodacom as being a perfect stepping stone, given its reputation and stature in the market.

Moreover, after 20 years in FMCG, I was wary of being pigeonholed. From the view of personal disruption, I felt being successful at Vodacom would be great for my self-confidence and my diversity of career options. I believed my learning curve in FMCG had plateaued and that I would not really be stretched if I remained in the beer and spirits market, no matter how senior my position.

The final reason in favour of joining Vodacom was that I believed the future lay in digital transformation. Uganda boasted a vibrant mobile money market and I noticed how people lived through their cellphones. I had witnessed the power of technology in transforming and improving lives, and wanted to have an impact in driving digitisation back in South Africa.

While for most multinationals the South African market is almost a rounding error in terms of revenue contribution, for Vodafone it was a significant player, so I felt assured that I could make a contribution that would be noticed. Although majority-owned by Vodafone, Vodacom was also listed on the JSE, so from the point of view of governance, board interaction and engagement with stakeholders, this would prepare me well for my ambition to be CEO of a listed company.

My journey at Vodacom began in September 2016 and I went through what I consider to be an exemplary induction and onboarding process. The company was clear about deliverables and expectations, as well as measurement of performance. I was also set up for success, including being sent on a six-week international induction where I visited various foreign markets to gather learnings on different aspects of the business. It was a great way to induct a recruit and got me to understand the culture and organisational language of the international units. This, I feel, is an often-overlooked aspect of induction.

The commercial side of Vodacom's business was divided into Business-to-Business (B2B), which handled corporate customers, and Business-to-Consumer (B2C), which focused on individual customers. My role was chief officer of the B2C unit, which made up about 70 per cent of Vodacom's business. I was also a group executive director of the Vodacom Group.

I was in charge of all things consumer-facing, which meant the Vodacom brand director and marketing officers reported to me, as did the heads of the customer base management team, customer care, up-selling and cross-selling, revenue management, loyalty, brand marketing and sponsorship, financial services, products and pricing. I, in turn, reported to the Vodacom CEO, Shameel Joosub.

My first year at Vodacom was full of learning. I had to understand the technicalities of how and where the telco made money, and where the further opportunities were. My task was to bring some innovative thinking to the picture so that Vodacom could improve on what already existed.

First, as with my term in Uganda, I needed to assess my team and ensure that I had the right people in the right roles. I made changes and hired in key positions, respecting continuity and recognising existing talent, while also promoting youngsters to create balance. I had to make sure the team was structured to be successful.

With a new team in place, I felt they would be able to deliver on the key strategies I'd identified through taking a close look at the consumer-facing business.

During my three years, Vodacom delivered strong results capped by a gain in market share overall, despite already being the number one player. I am a big fan of building for the future through innovation and some of the initiatives we set in motion during my time at Vodacom are still coming to fruition today.

At the time, telcos were at a critical juncture: voice revenues were under pressure from over-the-top services like WhatsApp and the #datamustfall movement was in full cry. This was something of a baptism by fire when I arrived in 2016. We needed to grow usage to make up for any shortfall in revenue from falling voice volumes and an industry-wide data price war. How could we reduce out-of-bundle data prices while protecting revenue?

As the largest market player, Vodacom was viewed as the proxy for negative sentiment over data pricing. We needed to protect the company's reputation and customer base while engaging with the regulator and undergoing price transformation.

We managed to gain market share and deliver compounded annual revenue growth of about 5 per cent in the face of this sentiment by being innovative – making use of big data, machine learning and artificial intelligence to enhance customer business management. We used machine learning to understand customer behaviour, habits and preferences to offer the right products at the right time and at a highly competitive price. The result was a slew of awards both internally and externally as a centre of excellence for big data. When you understand your customer better, you can anticipate their needs and offer solutions before they even ask questions. The evidence that Vodacom's brand benefitted from big data was clear.

During my tenure we also relaunched the Vodacom brand to bring the imagery and payoff line into alignment with the deployment of big data. Vodacom needed to become more than a telco by morphing into an end-to-end digital company. The transition was extremely important to the group's sustainability. Looking at East Africa's Safaricom as an example, that company was already generating 40 per cent of its revenue from mobile money and banking services thanks to a decision to avoid being boxed in as a voice and data service provider.

We had to be careful about positioning the brand in this context and although the change appeared subtle to some, it was significant in that the Vodacom network provided the power of connectivity. For our efforts Vodacom won several communications and advertising awards.

Strong brand positioning helped Vodacom weather the #datamustfall storm. Along with a public outcry over data prices, we faced an onslaught of aggressive competition for the number one market position. I also joined Vodacom at the time when MTN South Africa was accelerating investment in the network, ultimately winning the best network annual tests from multiple independent agencies, taking over from Vodacom. This added more competitive pressure; the onslaught from MTN was also led by my predecessor Godfrey Motsa, who not only understood us as a competitor but also recruited some of Vodacom's key talent. Regulatory and reputation pressure was also piling up, driven in part by the Competition Commission's pricing investigation and data pricing inquiry, and the extensive media coverage of the infamous 'Please call me' case of Mr Makate.

Part of our cost reduction drive included transforming how Vodacom engaged in sponsorships. One of the biggest challenges for many large organisations is maintaining control over sponsorships. At Vodacom, regional units would often act independently and there was no effective strategic control of how and where the brand's name was being used.

When I looked at Vodacom's sponsorship spend it was clear we were not getting a decent return on our investment and often lacked a clear rationale for engaging in some sponsorships. I insisted that sponsorships should be self-sustaining and integrate across our value chain. We came up with innovations like a market first in terms of sports-event insurance for fans with handsets, where the insurance would cover the particular day of a sports event where going to a stadium with a mobile phone was a high-risk activity.

There was a huge take-up of this service, and we launched contract and prepaid packages linked to sports franchises like the Blue Bulls and Kaizer Chiefs. These were affinity groups and we wanted to make sure revenue streams would also accrue to the teams through using the power of the combined brands. It led to activations like father-and-son outings and inspirational prizes to benefit contract users. We trialled this concept with the Blue Bulls, sending lucky winners to spend time with the players, but soon exported the idea from rugby to soccer.

The review of our sponsorship roster necessitated some tough contract discussions and asset exits – some of which involved millions of rands and constituted more than half of the budgets of asset owners. Bringing in performance measures and renegotiating contracts to achieve more favourable terms for Vodacom was tricky because it deviated from stipulated renewal terms, but this process provided a huge amount of learning for me in the area of stakeholder management.

I am pleased to say the outcome was a win-win scenario, because the asset owners were able to develop new revenue streams and business models based upon our renewed partnerships and Vodacom was also able to generate savings on existing sponsorships.

My FMCG background, where marketing budgets can be extremely tight, helped because FMCG companies are generally masters of consumer insights and understanding in optimising marketing effectiveness. This method of managing sponsorship assets persists at Vodacom after my departure.

Aligned with the sponsorships issue was the launch of Vodabucks, which was developed by my team and I and was implemented as a loyalty programme some months after my departure. I remember telling Shameel that I felt strongly that the company was not harnessing the power of a customer base of around 40 million effectively enough. The power of AI at that scale – understanding their needs, interests and behaviour – would allow us to launch what could instantly be the largest loyalty platform in South Africa.

Assembling the right team and conceiving of the Vodabucks setup was not easy, but we achieved global recognition within Vodafone by learning from the best programmes in the market and taking the best concepts from each of them. I have no doubt this programme will become a true champion for Vodacom, which illustrates the benefits of being the last mover in a space. Sometimes being first can work against you if your competitors are able to learn from your teething problems.

Adapt with pride and then scale fast. Can you do it better? If so, how do you differentiate your product? These are the questions that must be answered in a disciplined way. It is not always necessary to do something novel to be a success in the market. Successful new initiatives are rare. If you take something that isn't working optimally and you perfect it, it could be a winner for you.

Another of my highlights at Vodacom was the establishment of a Data Science team under my watch, reporting to my direct report. We were one of the first Vodafone group businesses and telcos in the world to set up a data analytics team of over forty professionals, working on case studies across the business. The team went on to win many global awards and saved Vodacom over half a billion rand, while generating incremental revenues of close to a billion rand across many portfolios – including financial services, contract upsell/saves and enterprise customers. The savings came from better network sites deployment, fraud reduction, automation, proactive maintenance of the network and many other similar areas.

As I had done in previous innovations, I looked for solutions from other markets which could be repurposed for the South African context. We took what worked and built on it so that we could leapfrog our competition. It is important to query even the strongest-held beliefs in an organisation. If you don't disrupt yourself, someone else will.

I'm inspired by things I see around me and one highlight of applying a successful example of digital transformation to Vodacom in South Africa came from my time in Uganda. When I lived in Uganda I – like everyone else in the country – went largely cashless because of the ease of using mobile payment solutions. You could pay for just about anything as long as the vendor had a mobile phone.

Even at an enterprise level, I used to boast to some of my colleagues back in South Africa that I was collecting money from distributors and taverns much quicker because as we delivered, they'd pay by mobile money. The situation in South Africa typically involved late payments, electronic fund transfers and the risk of cash robberies.

I thought financial services was also rife for disruption because of South Africa's high banking costs and the low level of insurance products held by the average person. The broker system has a lot to do with inflated costs, so I wondered how we could add value by disrupting the value chain.

With more than 40 million customers, Vodacom had a tremendous opportunity to determine personalised premiums based on machine learning and customer behaviour. We challenged ourselves to make a breakthrough and we had a lot of fun doing it. We brought in expertise from traditional banks, but also brought in people who were disruptors on a technical level.

With the help of Mariam Cassim, who was also an external recruit from the insurance industry, we grew the financial services business to become a high-growth area for the group. Her success in escalating the importance of financial services to group revenue led to her being promoted to group executive for financial services by the time of my departure.

A blend of talent is important for disruption and I was deliberate about it. You need traditionalists and new-age thinkers to build for the future. One of the best decisions we made was to place financial services into an acceleration unit, which Shameel and the board understood would perhaps take longer to provide a return on investment but which was a cornerstone to the future sustainability of the group.

It is sometimes necessary to make tough decisions about employees. As an external hire I was more easily able to see who was adding value and who was not, and my policy is that there is no room for passengers. We exited some employees on the basis of performance or strategic misalignment, which was difficult, but those who remained raised their game and feared that complacency would lose them their jobs.

Suddenly, top talent from outside the financial services acceleration unit expressed interest in getting involved. This was unheard of previously, in the days of financial services at a telco being limited to device insurance. We rewarded employees for delivering on their KPIs and took measurements seriously.

In turn, Vodacom branched out to providing sports event insurance, life insurance and funeral policies, as well as consolidating municipal accounts and providing value-added deals linked to Vodabucks. These services were opened to non-Vodacom customers through the app, which allowed us to build relationships and tell potential customers about relevant products in our ecosystem.

Then we got into lending. We took a commoditised product like airtime advances and analysed it, realising it held a lot of potential. We grew lending revenue tenfold in three years through providing airtime overdrafts. We also extended lending services to informal businesses and SMEs, using big data to de-risk the loan book.

Vodacom's ambition in this space remains massive as a trendsetter and the growth has been mind-blowing. It required understanding, patience and tolerating some failures, but that is the nature of innovation.

Though I was enjoying this series of successes in bringing new thinking to the consumer business division, I was humbled by being asked to take on additional responsibilities within the group. Being entrusted with greater responsibility is a leading indicator of how well you are regarded and how valuable the company considers you to be, since it is an opportunity for you to showcase your capacity.

These are opportunities to learn and demonstrate leadership, and I believe many people make the mistake of refusing extra responsibility for no additional pay. Pushing back means failing to show that you can be a bigger leader than your current role allows and that you are not interested in the health of the broader organisation. I consider my readiness to assume more responsibility as my signature, though there is the caveat that one still needs to deliver on one's regular job.

Shameel would sometimes be travelling for an extended period, or be on leave, and would ask me to step in as acting group CEO. Obviously, I would need to communicate with him regarding any key decisions, but he would delegate authority and governance rights to me in dealing with the board and its chair. While I had run UBL, this was a beast on a different scale.

For me to be at a point where Shameel trusted me with his responsibilities, within six months of joining the industry and with no stipulation that he should choose me, was a fantastic endorsement of my performance. I may not have known all of the intricacies some of my colleagues did, but one of my strengths is building relationships quickly and I felt this had paid off.

Stepping into Shameel's shoes every so often gave me a tantalising taste of what it would be like to run a JSE-listed entity, even though the role of a CEO can be cumbersome and extremely demanding of one's time. It also gave me the opportunity to build relationships with external stakeholders who were not my natural audiences. My knowledge of the business was accelerated through preparing for interviews, speeches and discussions with other parties.

A highlight related to such additional responsibility came towards the end of 2017, when one of my executive colleagues who was in charge of commercial operations resigned. Commercial operations was the business unit responsible for managing the customer experience and employed about 5 000 people, including 4 000 call centre staff who handled 3 million calls per month. The backbone of the customer experience, 'cops' ensured a smooth process from onboarding to fulfilment. Though Vodacom had found a replacement, the new executive would be coming in from abroad only six months after the departure of the incumbent. Shameel asked me to take over for that period and ensure that it continued to function effectively.

This was a tremendous challenge because I had never run a call centre or customer service department, but I saw it as an important caretaking role because the effective functioning of cops had a great bearing on customer churn, which fed directly into the unit I was leading.

For those six months I split my time between two offices, two personal assistants and two sets of staff, alternating days. Even though I was not technically grounded in what cops did, I was relentless about stretching the team and demanding improved outcomes. If you know which KPIs show you're going in the right direction, that really simplifies things. I'm a good listener and I like to empower people, but I also follow through strictly to make sure we deliver.

It's an important lesson that has been delivered time and again in my career: you can't be intimidated by a function not being related to your technical background. You can still find solutions if something is at stake. Failure to deliver must have consequences. If you understand what the issues are, you can solve a problem at its source.

Most leaders tend to stay in their lane instead of thinking about the system as a whole. This is partly a result of the way employees are trained, which can box us in. Business is an integrated system and you can be much more effective in your role when you understand how to get the best out of people in other divisions.

Curiosity and an attitude of wanting to learn fast to appreciate where others are coming from provides a great boost to corporate relationships and effectiveness.

I had to learn very quickly when I was appointed as the executive in charge of digital transformation at Vodacom – a long-term strategy of transitioning from being a voice-and-data telco to becoming a full-service digital company. South Africa fell into the second phase of transitions, so we could learn from the experience of developed markets, in conjunction with a global consulting firm acting as a guide. My task was to get Vodacom to transition from many manual processes to being completely digital and contactless, using technology to power customer touchpoints, especially.

People are creatures of habit, even if the new ways of doing things can make their lives easier. I was intent on changing everything in a digital-first strategy – right down to the way employees worked in the office.

A massive breakthrough was to set up cross-functional working, which eliminated the old business unit silos. In a silo setup, most employees have no idea where they fit in or why they do what they do. In an agile, cross-functional setup, everyone working on a project is in the same room and they report to the project lead.

We set up squads and tribes, which were all output-focused instead of function-focused. The first tribe created fell under my leadership and was designed to improve the customer journey through online channels. It resulted in a more than 400 per cent sales increase by destroying existing channel blockages.

An important lesson from this time was that adaptation and innovation will always include a certain number of failures, but especially in a multinational it is vital to absorb experiences from other markets to avoid repeating mistakes.

When we set up the new working structure we looked beyond the telco sector for models. Ultimately, a consumer is a consumer, a customer is a customer. Your customers don't judge you according to other players in your sector; they judge you as a customer of all businesses from which they buy, using the same standards.

To provide digital transformation sponsors with learnings across sectors we were taken to visit organisations like ING, renowned for its change in culture, and to Silicon Valley to see the likes of Spotify and the customer journeys they had designed.

Digital transformation was much easier for new companies with no legacy systems, so what I needed to do was create an environment where Vodacom could act quicker, correct course quicker, improve decision-making and bring clarity of roles and purpose.

Driving the change to becoming customer-led was what really instilled the agility Vodacom needed. Good leaders identify game changers ahead of the curve and back them. There is skill in picking the next big thing. That can be transformational in anyone's career.

There is also a skill in picking the next big star. I am passionate about talent development and particularly keen on youngsters who have not yet been contaminated by ideas of what a corporate should be. I am a huge believer in nourishing young talent by allowing them to take on responsibility.

The world changes quickly – whether we're talking Takealot in South Africa or Google, Facebook, Airbnb and Uber internationally, most of these corporate giants are not yet 20 years old. They exist primarily because young people use them. Young people buy online, they pay online, they behave differently from people who run a typical business. They have money to spend and they are going to be your consumers for a long time, defining the future of your business. Yet they remain misunderstood. How can you sell something to someone you don't understand?

I encouraged Vodacom to think in this way – to evolve young talent in their twenties and accelerate their development into key positions. At the very least, to listen to them. To do this, I championed two initiatives at Vodacom, both started during my time there. I enjoyed a close relationship with the company's group chief HR officer, Matimba

Mbungela, so I was able to influence him and share my thoughts. I was appointed an executive sponsor of the Vodacom Discover graduate programme.

Many organisations run graduate programmes, and of course I was a product of such a programme at P&G. I didn't want this programme to be seen as an initiative of HR. Rather, it needed to be owned by all departments to ensure its success, since its purpose was to provide the talent pool from which we could draw future leaders and ensure sustainability.

My way of being an active citizen within the organisation was to act as mentor and coach to help graduates learn the language and culture of the business and to develop their capabilities. Today's graduates are so much smarter than we were – and have no excuse not to be. In my time, graduating in 1995, computers were not widely available, internet penetration was low and you had to pay top dollar to gain access to learning materials.

Today, the internet is a melting pot of information and access is relatively cheap. University platforms are often zero-rated by telcos and a lot of material has been democratised by digitalisation, made available by donor and developmental organisations. You can learn to do anything online.

Such access to information has built the capacity of today's graduates. What took us years to learn can now be absorbed quickly. Today's kids may be able to learn from our experience, but their capacity to learn is greater than ours was and I am frustrated by corporate systems that do not recognise this sea change. I think kids could complete their schooling in eight years. There are just so many better ways of delivering instruction.

There is much I would like to challenge about the way things are done today. I was able to do a lot as an executive sponsor for the programme – fostering relationships with universities, leveraging my internal contacts to get people to talk to graduates and inspire them, and to accelerate their development.

We held focus groups at Vodacom and young employees were often taken aback that someone was actually asking for their opinions. The company had been losing a lot of graduates, which had been dismissed as a result of millennial habits, but I was not happy with this explanation and believed it was a lazy way of thinking. It prevented us from dealing with the real issues. We had to delve deeper into exit interviews, which resulted in improved engagement and retention.

When young people were given opportunities to take on more responsibility at Vodacom, we were almost always surprised by their capacity to deliver. Inspired by the youth parliament in which I had participated, I suggested establishing a parallel youth executive committee, where employees in their twenties could provide the voice of young people on the same issues our exco would wrestle with. We'd ask them to make their own decisions, with corresponding senior exco members as mentors and coaches. Not everything suggested was adopted, but it ensured robust debate and provided an alternative voice that represented customers who could not be in the room, which was very useful.

HR is simply a facilitator. Talent ownership rests with the line manager and the business unit, because ultimately talent is deployed into those units. A leader should take an active interest in finding the right people for his or her team, then get actively involved in performance management and rewards. Too much lip service is paid to people being a business's most important asset. Practices are where the truth lies. It can transform a business and has worked wonders during my career.

If you want to compete with digital unicorns you cannot have an exco whose average age is much older than your customers – it's that simple. Grounded in diplomacy and respect, I have never been ashamed to raise issues that make people uncomfortable. False unity and homogeneity will not take a business forward. Look for diversity in thought and action.

While disruption – whether in technology or people – within Vodacom was a great deal of fun and I found it exciting, it also ultimately led to my departure from the company. While I was being inundated with new concepts and new ways of doing business, I saw that we were really just scratching the surface of what was possible. There was so much more

I wanted and needed to understand to position myself as a thought leader. How would such changes affect the local economy and South Africa at large? I was grappling with ever-larger questions and began to think I could only achieve greater understanding by taking a sabbatical.

What better way to continue this learning curve than to be exposed to various industries through sitting on boards and being part of a leading consulting firm which held the expertise and capabilities to research digital transformation in depth? During my sabbatical year, I couldn't help wondering just how much I could have achieved in the traditional businesses I'd led if I'd known then what I know now. But I could never have learnt so much while working.

7
TAKING A NO-GAP YEAR

In March 2019 I left Vodacom without having lined up another job. This period of what I like to call 'productive rest' lasted until 1 May 2020, when I returned to corporate life as CEO of GE Southern Africa. Exactly how stepping out of corporate life for more than a year worked in my favour has perplexed many of my friends and associates, but I believe my reasoning is validated by the result.

I left a high-paying job in a group executive role at one of the country's top-ten listed companies by market capitalisation, and which is a sought-after employer in a growing tech industry, to take some time off. Was I crazy?

Vodacom is an incredible business, with a supportive majority shareholder in Vodafone, high profit margins and the ability to make a difference in people's lives. It's hard to ignore the virtues of such a company – not to mention the highly talented and diverse executive teams running the business.

The truth is that I realised I wasn't enjoying working at Vodacom as much as I thought I would. I am at my best when I have absolute accountability that comes with a CEO position. Leading a division of a larger group meant I wasn't running the show. The consumer division was the largest among the group's units, but I felt that my preferred maverick approach to decision making, risk taking, innovation and speed of execution was stifled by the group's structures. Thankfully this has since changed – as of July 2020, when Vodacom Group became a standalone region representing all of Vodafone's Africa businesses, with Vodacom's Group CEO reporting directly to the Vodafone Global CEO and becoming a global executive committee member. This effectively took away a layer in the reporting structure of the Vodacom group, bringing it closer to decision makers and improving the speed of those decisions while reducing the significant costs of a regional structure – which, in my view, added minimal value.

When I have been fully accountable for results my speed of decision making has worked in my favour. At Diageo I had a lot of freedom because my portfolio was different from that of a typical multinational – 60 per cent of my profits came from Ugandan brands that did not feature anywhere else in Diageo, so I was given an opportunity to shine, with no global brand team's intervention and limitations that can come with that.

With hindsight, all the roles I've held where I excelled featured little scrutiny and a lot of freedom. I was typically running programmes that were new and required best practice to be established, rather than followed. I consider myself a compliant leader, but I have never sought the type of role that involves working on untouchable, unchangeable big brands. Crown jewels seldom offer much freedom in their handling.

I needed to get back into a role with greater responsibility quickly, but my boss at Vodacom – group CEO Shameel Joosub – was still a young and energetic person doing a great job. His position was not going to be within reach for some time. My options were either to leave South Africa to get into another smaller role as CEO with parent group Vodafone, or stick it out in a divisional role for longer. Neither of these appealed to me because I had just returned from seven years abroad, during which I'd lost my father. I wanted to be back home, particularly to be close to my mother, who was approaching the last years of her life.

It was time to make a tough decision. Naturally, I received a lot of calls from executive search firms for opportunities, and one listed company searching for a CEO seemed a great fit from the outset. I went through the selection process, made it through successive cuts of the shortlist and ended up being one of two candidates for the role. This was an incredible journey which took seven months.

The executive search firm told me to expect that vying for such a position as my first CEO role in a listed company would mean potentially not being selected, but that I should treat the exercise as a learning curve – the role was a high-profile one and the selection process extremely competitive. I would be experiencing what a top-class board demands of a chosen leader.

In my experience, such processes always begin with the chairman, followed by a nominations committee and then presentations to the full board and major shareholders. I found this exciting and was surprised to hear that I had been recommended for the role. I was ready, and I had fully reawakened my longing for the independence and excitement of being a leader.

Suddenly my sense of anticipation was shattered by the news that the board had discovered acts of malfeasance, which had left the business in worse shape than expected. Skeletons began to tumble out of closets and the scope of the CEO's role changed to become that of a turnaround strategist – a seasoned CEO on their third or fourth rotation.

It was a bittersweet outcome. I knew I'd been recommended for the role and lucky to escape taking what suddenly seemed like a poisoned chalice, but I was effectively back to square one after a long interview process. I had become fully immersed in this company and I had envisioned myself executing on my strategic plans. My heart was no longer in my job at Vodacom.

I consulted with my mentor, my coaches and the executive search firm. Despite my inclination to be a maverick leader, I strongly recommend consultation as a means of improving decision making. The search firm was adamant that my profile was suitable for a CEO role and any further time I spent at Vodacom in a divisional executive role would not add value. I was growing frustrated and decided the best course of action for me would be to take some time off.

I could take a sabbatical, learn new skills, relax and enjoy myself while I waited for the right opportunity, but this was a daunting prospect. It meant giving up a salary and being unsure of what would come next in either months or years. I knew I would have to find a way to keep busy, stay relevant to potential employers and take care of my family.

One thing that made me more comfortable with the idea was that in my role at Vodacom I had the good fortune to travel extensively. I had been asked to lead digital transformation within the group from end to end, since it needed to be informed by commercial viability in the consumer-facing business. My travels took in Vodafone subsidiaries in the UK, Germany, Italy, Spain, India, Portugal, Egypt and Turkey. Throughout the information-gathering process I was working with a top-three global consulting firm that was appointed to help us in our journey. This made me realise that I had learnt an incredible amount in three years and was being challenged as a business leader – how prepared was I to take advantage of all this new technology? I needed to take time to reflect on my career and carefully consider what I wanted to do next as I passed the age of 40.

I decided I would apply discontinuity for exponential growth. I used to think of sabbaticals as a white-people thing – that they were the ones who could afford to take time off for gap years or travel, while the rest of us worked continuously until retirement. My family had certainly followed that path. Suddenly, however, I felt exhausted and the thought of doing nothing for a while began to appeal to me.

I had worked for 23 years non-stop. When I took time off, I'd go to the beach with my family but spend my time responding to emails and phone calls. My chosen parenting model, as with many successful professionals, was to outsource my functions to private tutors, a driver with a dedicated car for my kids' transport, and other hired help. On sabbatical, I'd be able to attend my kids' school performances or sports events. I'd be able to help them with their homework. Up to that point, it had been difficult to balance the careers of two hard-working parents and the needs of our kids, despite our best intentions. My salary and savings were large enough that I could afford to take a year or two of not working and survive, so I thought why not?

I did the unthinkable and disrupted myself. I resigned and intended my first three months to entail some international travel and attending some conferences to catch up on global leadership best practice, as well as some executive education courses here and there. Then I could come back to the corporate world and see what happens. That was the plan.

I knew I had a low boredom threshold and needed high-energy commitments to prevent intellectual frustration, so I was determined to remain open to all possibilities, whether furthering my education or giving my time to those who needed it. As fate would have it, this time turned out to be extremely productive – I don't remember another 15-month period in my life in which I learnt as much.

Although I ended up being very busy, I had the luxury of being in control of my own time. If I wanted to start work later in the day, I could. If I wanted to travel, I didn't have to schedule leave at a time that was convenient. I was busy when I wanted to be. The self-determination was extremely empowering.

By April, I had five new roles. I was recruited into four non-executive directorships in different industries, some of which were new to me. I sat on the divisional board of a diversified listed financial services group, a reputable South African listed real estate investment company and two Ethos Private Equity portfolio companies. Private equity was new and exciting to me. To my surprise and delight, I was asked to be chairman of one of these companies – South Africa's biggest mobile accessories player. Already my decision to step away from corporate life seemed to be paying dividends.

Then I was approached by one of the three largest management consulting firms in the world, Boston Consulting Group (BCG), to be a senior advisor. This was an incredible role because their standards are so high – to become an advisor generally meant being a CEO and respected industry leader who could bring proposals and recommendations to client businesses to add value. In short, it was like being hired as an in-house executive for BCG's clients. It also entailed giving practitioner advice and guidance to the managing directors and senior partners at BCG, an extremely intellectually stimulating role.

I was to become one of 200 senior advisors around the world; being trusted with such responsibility was humbling. The role required five to ten days a month working across the consumer goods, technology, media and telecommunications sectors in Sub-Saharan Africa.

While these interviews and meetings had kept me busy enough, I also spent a week at Stanford University in California, invited by its business school thanks to someone I had worked with previously and who was now involved with the university. I became involved in organising the Stanford Africa Week, which culminated in a conference where the focus was on US–African business relations. I was asked to be a speaker, panellist and judge for the start-up competition, which brought together entrepreneurs and venture financiers in the tech space.

I felt like I was back at school – curious, open to learning, hunting down opportunities. I could stay as long as I wanted to, since I had no work to rush back to, and I turned the visit into a learning experience.

The lesson from this experience was to become comfortable with ambiguity and uncertainty. The importance of an ability to deal with the unknown is an underappreciated leadership trait. When I was invited to Stanford I decided to extend my trip by another week after the official programme, without an agenda. Through the contacts I'd made at the conference, I met up with some incredible entrepreneurs and venture capital financiers, and was drawn into their way of thinking. It was inspiring.

I then toured Silicon Valley privately, where I found an incubation hub called Plug and Play and met their now director for Africa, Karen Airola. At the time they had no business interests on the continent but wanted to enter. We've since had conversations where I advised them on an entry strategy and they've appointed a country director. I continue to be part of this journey, and that all came about through a chance meeting.

Travelling and networking is important – the US trip didn't just raise my profile as a panellist at Stanford; it increased my market value thanks to new perceptions about my capabilities. All of a sudden I had people wanting to know what I was up to and how I came to be involved there. These are the kinds of opportunities I would never have been given had I been working full-time in a corporate role.

That week propelled me and my personal brand onto international platforms and resulted in further requests to speak and be involved at similar events in other African countries. I still value that Stanford experience and it continues to contribute to my profile.

In November 2019 I was lined up as a keynote speaker and panel facilitator at a three-day event which featured 300 CEOs and CMOs together with agency leaders across disciplines. The event hosted a series of conversations and experiences focused on burning issues and new ideas for the marketing industry for its clients across the world. This is a highly sought-after event and guests in South Africa included Absa, Amazon, BBC, Google, Facebook, Standard Bank, MTN, Vodacom, Singularity University, Unilever, Liberty and other top organisations.

I spoke on two topics: about winning in Africa, focusing on why so many businesses were failing on the rest of the continent and reflecting on withdrawals by the likes of Pick n Pay, Woolworths, Tiger Brands, Group Five and others from certain markets, and about the future of market research. Calling it 'Research Is Dead', I gave what I thought was a provocative talk about how the research and consumer insights industry could become another Blackberry, Nokia or Blockbuster, or at the least suffer what Uber did to the taxi industry due to advances in artificial intelligence and real-time behavioural data.

I earned some fantastic reviews, which led to at least three non-conflicting private consulting jobs. What I particularly enjoy about thought leadership is how it enhances one's learning, because to be a respected thought leader you need to stay informed and ahead of the curve on the chosen topic.

Back home, my board roles were rounding out my corporate learnings. Through my involvement on the four boards I was able to focus on the areas for improvement that were highlighted by the executive search company during my recruitment for the CEO role. The areas in which I had less experience than my competitors were stakeholder management and dealing with a board. I needed to become well versed in corporate governance and my decision to actively seek board appointments was driven by this goal.

Becoming a board member had the additional benefit of being able to watch from the other side of the table. I got to see how experienced CEOs in different industries managed their relationships with their boards. I was learning more about what boards expect from CEOs and how CEOs fulfil those expectations.

I was also gaining experience in managing and optimising a balance sheet – another area in which I needed to prove my ability, since I had worked mainly for multinationals that were listed offshore. A core competence of a CEO is selling assets to reduce debt, making funding decisions, issuing capital, acquiring assets and generally ensuring the sustainability of the organisation.

A CEO needs to actively drive balance sheet activity. With that in mind, working with a private equity company was enlightening because the main goal was achieving a maximum asset price at exit. I was adding to my own value proposition at the same time.

I had been worried about my phone going quiet once I resigned from Vodacom because I had heard many horror stories of what happens when you are no longer perceived to be in an influential position, but my opportunistic strategy allowed me to seize several opportunities quickly. I was amazed and humbled by how many people wanted my time – and by how many were equally willing to give me their time.

We don't always need to wait for answers. The 80/20 rule in business – where we should be able to make decisions confidently when we know 80 per cent of the facts – applies to our lives too. Not everything will fall into place before we can take a leap.

In the worst-case scenario, I would get some rest and use some of my savings. I knew that if the year turned out to be a terrible idea, I still had a strong record of delivering in corporate setups across different geographies and industries – I would be able to get a job. My advice is to just take the step if you can – claim back your time and have some fun in achieving your goals. For me, it was all about rediscovering the fun element of working.

I was also investing in my future. Part of the reason being recruited to boards made sense to me was because this is what I wanted to do when I retired from full-time corporate work. I look forward to being able to provide guidance and share my experience as an external voice when the time comes.

Sitting on various boards across several industries has also allowed me to gain a broader view of leadership, since being on the board is akin to sitting on the sidelines as a coach rather than being a player focused on positional play. I have learnt a lot about problem solving from executive teams, about how board members are recruited and how a corporation's governing bodies interact.

My first taste of non-executive board activity coincided with some high-profile corporate governance failures making media headlines – whether at state-owned enterprises like SAA and Eskom, at listed companies such as Steinhoff and Tongaat Hulett or indeed governance failures at international consultancies and audit firms like Deloitte, KPMG, McKinsey & Company, and Bain & Company. The reaction of regulators was to move to make board members more personally liable for governance, because significant amounts of money had been lost and questions were now being asked about the effectiveness of boards.

Board members were becoming worried about issues such as independence, fees and performance, and recruiters were demanding experience and commercial understanding. This presented an interesting dynamic while sitting on boards – we had to unlearn certain practices and be part of the change under increased scrutiny.

It also taught me more about the responsibilities of a CEO, because corporate governance failures had destroyed the life savings of so many South Africans. A kind of revolution in corporate governance and leadership was required to avoid further devastation. I wanted to make sure that I was aligned with all the new best practice when the time came for me to lead.

The other crash course in leadership responsibility during this time was forced upon all of us by the extraordinary events related to the COVID-19 pandemic. The volatility, uncertainty and unprecedented complexity of leading an organisation through that time required almost constant crisis management. Board meetings moved from being quarterly to weekly and called for a great deal of board member involvement.

COVID-19 brought about previously unheard-of circumstances, like successful tenant retailers suddenly being unable to pay rent to highly leveraged property investment companies. The industry's dynamics changed completely and suddenly. Nobody had modelled the health protocols we had to put in place before, insurance claims skyrocketed, cash flow and profitability trends were utterly disrupted.

One benefit I had was being able to draw learnings from various sectors, and particularly from the Ethos stable, which held a large pool of CEOs and chairpersons with whom I could compare notes. This provided a richness of learnings and an understanding of the linkages between sectors and companies to help provide leadership through a severely challenging time.

In a new normal, you cannot approach a situation that has changed forever by applying what you've done before. The only way to emerge as a winner is to be agile and prepared, with a restructured operating model. Businesses that continued to grow and thrive during COVID-19's decimation of the economy were businesses that innovated. Complaining is easy – my attitude was that, if a business can still thrive during such times, why isn't it *your* business?

While sitting on boards during such a crisis provided an exponential learning curve, I also took some formal education to complement my experiential learning. Bain & Company ran board governance training in South Africa, with international learnings provided by the UK and Singapore and distilled into a course called The Great Board. This course covered board composition, creating an effective board from a team dynamics point of view, recruiting board members, setting the right agenda, the relationship between the chair, board and CEO, managing dynamics, maintaining independence and tenure.

Stepping down from a board is something we don't often think about. It is easy to become obsessed with raking in board fees to make a good living, and to be dependent on these roles. You can end up selling your soul and compromising your integrity and reputation.

During this period I considered my board roles to be an education, so I was not concerned about remuneration – in fact, I barely expected to be paid for what I was doing, considering the benefits I was gaining.

Being involved with a consulting firm meant experiencing a business-to-business environment, which was new to me. I had been customer-facing for many years, but things change when your customer is another business. The guidance BCG provided tended to be for high-value projects, such as an overhaul of the client's customer service structures, digital transformation or key investment decisions.

Obtaining an external point of view was exciting because I had a high regard for consultants – not least because my wife had spent five years at McKinsey & Company and further time at Accenture. I admired and respected the work she had done with these firms. As an executive I had also greatly benefitted from working with top consulting firms as a client lead for high-impact projects across all the businesses where I had worked.

The problem was that I liked to get my hands dirty. I didn't view myself as someone who would guide from a distance, telling someone else what to do. I wanted to see the moving parts, experience the implementation. I also didn't fit the typical profile of a consultant – in my experience, consultants were the A+ students who were articulate and polished.

I was fascinated by the opportunity to become associated with big brands and the glamour of their major projects, and humbled to be able to contribute practical guidance where BCG had realised an academic approach should be blended with real-world expertise.

BCG wanted me to assist in my areas of strength and interests, particularly in consumer goods and in Sub-Saharan Africa. This was a space I understood in a multinational context, so I was glad to be able to apply so many career learnings. I was also able to leverage my networks of contacts and relationships to help BCG win multimillion-dollar projects. Consulting involves long lead times and a lot of influence, which was new to me, and exciting. I found myself invited to give keynote addresses at various companies on digital transformation, monetisation and business model defence, which was extremely stimulating.

This allowed me to learn a great deal from case studies of offshore industry players. Watching the young consultants delivering presentations felt like going back to school for me. The consulting business model was changing fast – firms like BCG didn't just want to tell clients what to do; they wanted to partner in joint ventures to create new revenue streams. Effectively, this meant putting money behind what would previously have been theoretical ideas. BCG established a Ventures division, which would search for investment opportunities. It felt good to be able to bring projects to the table and I left a healthy pipeline behind after 14 months.

I had last completed a formal qualification in 2004, when I got my MBA. In this year of multifaceted learning I wanted something to show for it by way of accreditation. I believe not having direct experience is no barrier – you don't need to know everything to succeed in a new context – but in executive coaching it felt necessary to have a certificate.

There are many executive coaches in the marketplace, usually former HR professionals, assessment analysts, strategists or industrial psychologists. They have exploited the gap by supporting executives, and I had been exposed to their one-on-one services in various roles.

I remember my first executive coach, Charles Mead, a director at UK-based leadership consultancy YSC, very well. Diageo recognised that it's lonely at the top when you're paid to solve problems and provided us with this outlet. The board puts you under pressure to find solutions, as do unions and employees. It can be difficult to find help or guidance, or to admit there are things you don't know.

When they feel vulnerable most executives turn to their spouses, because it is human nature to want to confide in someone. I believe it is not necessary to have been an executive to become an executive coach, just as it is not necessary to have been a great player to become a great coach in soccer, for example. Context and experience are important – current executives could do with more CEOs who have walked the path making themselves available as coaches.

Coaching is different from mentorship, and I believe doing it well requires training. Those who have succeeded have qualifications because being a coach demands new capabilities. I have a passion for helping executives to be successful and for advisory work, which was a flame fanned by my role as a consultant and as a board member. My retirement plan involves helping leaders to thrive and win, using my experience to help others deliver better results.

I researched the right institution for executive coaching and spoke with those who had taken such courses for testimonials. Ultimately, I decided to do a six-week course through the Gordon Institute of Business Science (GIBS), which required 100 hours of practical coaching time to achieve accreditation.

It was fascinating being back in a lecture room, with 40 of us trying to be professional coaches. There was lots of laughter and nervousness, but I was focused on refining my understanding of how to stand on the other side of the fence, so to speak.

My relationships at Vodacom came in handy for my 100 hourly sessions of coaching to build up my practical experience – I was given a coaching contract with 6 executives at 12 sessions per person, which built up more than 70 per cent of my requirement.

I avoid burning bridges in what can be a small corporate leadership community and was grateful to be able to go back to Vodacom as a supplier. I enjoyed seeing people grow and half the trainees I coached moved to bigger roles. We maintain tight relationships today.

With hindsight, that qualification should have capped what was an extremely busy year, despite my intentions to indulge in some rest. But there were still further highlights to come on the business and philanthropic fronts.

I grew up in retail and have always loved the sector. Through my involvement with Ethos I was introduced to the AutoZone car parts business, which operates as a distributor and seller of automotive components. After working closely with the company's leadership, I approached them to open a franchise in Rolle, Bushbuckridge, at my parents' old premises. A petrol station had been developed on the site, in a shopping centre on the outskirts of the village, and after conducting some market research I felt there was an opportunity for a spares shop given the number of old vehicles in the town. I believed we could bring a strong brand to the area.

After much location verification, assessment and discussion I was allowed to invest, with my sister running the business. What makes me proud is that we employed eight people who were previously unemployed. They're now able to feed their families and earn salaries operating the shop. My family effectively owns the business, and I am able to provide support remotely by checking on accounts and giving guidance to the team from Johannesburg. I was thrilled not only to create employment but also to continue my parents' legacy in retail on that site, using my own savings to make a difference in other people's lives.

During the year I also used my spare capacity to accept an executive role as CFO in the Pretoria chapter of the YPO, a society for those who have become CEOs before the age of 45. This role has given me access to the organisation's other members, and I get to travel around the world to attend YPO functions. This proved useful during the COVID-19 disruption because we have been able to support each other through webinars. It's an interesting blend, with about 60 per cent of the members being founders and owners of businesses and 40 per cent being in the corporate space.

We learn a lot from each other and entrepreneurs are well known for avoiding waste. They try to do as much as they can by themselves in the absence of large budgets and big teams, and this aligns closely with my passion for the building blocks of corporate entrepreneurship – risk aversion, diversification of skills, cost efficiency, innovation and creativity. A lot can be achieved if you approach a corporate entity with a founder's mindset.

Finally, I was able to dedicate some of my available time to the African Philanthropy Forum (APF), which encourages high net worth individuals and organisations in Africa to spend part of their wealth on philanthropic projects. There may not be as much wealth in Africa as is present in other continents, but we could do better in redistributing our wealth. The objective is to reach Africa's high net worth individuals with the right proposition and provide the right channels. The APF has a very strong board, including Yvonne Chaka Chaka, Tsitsi Masiyiwa and others from across the continent who understand the needs, and they do great work.

Closer to home, my wife and I revived the Saseka Foundation, a non-profit organisation in which we play voluntary roles in advisory, strategic, marketing and eventing capacities to make a difference in poverty eradication. Through the foundation, we set up a free computer training facility in Bushbuckridge, which uses laptops with high-speed LTE connections and a full-time teacher to help local students overcome the challenges posed by school closures as a result of COVID-19. For most rural students, access to computers and internet connectivity is out of reach, so this facility helps maintain access to the curriculum through remote learning – especially for those in matric.

We also prepared meals and distributed them in Gauteng townships for kids who were cut off from school feeding schemes during the pandemic. This work has been extremely fulfilling and has allowed us to ensure that the meals reach intended recipients because we are closely involved.

Although it took many unexpected twists and turns, my year of productive rest allowed me to do what was in my heart, on my own terms and in my own time. Through doing all of that, I was able to make a difference in the lives of others.

8
A B2B ADVENTURE

I am a believer in lifelong learning and development in parallel with my journey to a leadership position. Whether to become adept at dealing with digital transformation as a business leader, to delve deeper into the nuances of good corporate governance as a consultant, or to bolster my risk management skills as a non-executive director, I have sought every opportunity to expand my skill set.

The COVID-19 pandemic's arrival in South Africa in 2020 accelerated my personal learnings at a time when I was taking the reins at GE. The self-assessment of my achievements during this time therefore goes beyond mere financial figures.

My time at GE has been fascinating – especially because it was not a position I actively sought or considered. I was enjoying myself, a year into board roles as a non-executive director, and already being taken on a steep learning curve by Octodec, given the way the real estate investment trust had been affected by lockdown restrictions.

I was busy: BCG clients were looking for advice to help them navigate through unprecedented cash flow interruptions, Octodec's tenants were in a battle to survive and negotiations were constant. When the call came about the GE opportunity from an executive search firm, I considered a potential move to be premature at first since I was fully committed to my existing roles and really wanted to see through a sabbatical that had just been too busy; part of me was still hoping to slow down somehow.

Only one year into my board tenures, I was concerned about deserting my posts without a sustained record of achievement. However, after several discussions with the firm and GE, I was assured of flexibility to continue with my board commitments. As long as I delivered on my work and objectives GE would be happy, which was an attractive proposition.

There were several aspects of the GE role that grabbed my attention. First, I love and thrive on turnaround situations. Typically, coming into a business under pressure, you are allowed to be innovative, try new methods and push boundaries. I dislike arriving at an organisation to find naysayers who resist changing tack because an idea has been tried before and failed, or makes them uneasy. Nothing rules out trying again today what failed yesterday. An idea can be executed incorrectly or be ahead of its time. Timing matters.

Negative energy, especially in companies that have enjoyed a measure of success by taking one path without exploring others, can make the difference between double-digit and triple-digit growth. Why deny yourself the possibility of constant renovation, innovation and reinvention?

Companies in crisis are usually much more open to change, and it was no secret that, even prior to 2020, GE had experienced turbulence globally. The previous CEO, John Flannery, had left after just 18 months at the helm, and for the first time in the company's history of 129 years an external leader was brought in to arrest the slide.

Lawrence 'Larry' Culp bucked the trend of GE growing its leaders from within. With 30 000 employees globally, the company did not lack talent and had produced celebrity CEOs such as Jack Welch, but when GE lost its way the board decided the group needed new ideas and inspiration. Larry was lecturing at Harvard. He'd retired as CEO of Danaher, a smaller business, but sat on the GE board, and understood the issues the company was facing. He was asked to step out of retirement to guide GE out of the doldrums with a five-year agreement, but after just two years that agreement was extended by a further two years.

Larry has made changes, brought a fresh perspective to GE, and hired external talent as CFO, HR director as well as the heads of the group's aviation and health businesses. Larry is a sharp, bold executive who is performing well as the global CEO. GE is comfortably in recovery as a global giant thanks to his leadership. He has done a phenomenal job of modernising GE.

Despite GE's well-publicised problems and the massive restructuring exercise driven by Larry, it is a mistake and disrespectful to assume that a business under pressure is uniformly weak. GE's heritage and iconic status have endured, not simply because of a change in leadership. The blend of old and new, internal and external, was exciting for me and defined the approach I would take with GE Southern Africa going forward.

The second aspect of the position that excited me was the quantum leap in fields of knowledge I would have to absorb. From my background in FMCG and telecommunications, joining a business specialising in renewable energy, healthcare and aviation promised a sustained period of learning that would enrich me personally. I had no experience in any of these fields, and it spoke volumes about GE's intentions that they approached me to run the business. They were obviously prepared to step out of their comfort zone to find new ideas.

To lead a team of such astute and experienced professionals, as a commercial specialist, is a thrill for me. I ask the stupid questions, but those can often draw the best answers and unlock possibilities. As I have mentioned elsewhere in this book, businesses like Facebook, Uber and Airbnb were started and run by people who did not work in media, logistics or hospitality, respectively. Yet they have become immensely successful by asking some fairly basic questions.

Naiveté can lead to breakthroughs, especially if they are focused on the only experience that matters – that of the customers. How are you taking your customer on a journey that meets their expectations and provides delight along the way? The blend of external best practice and thinking with engineering skill and experience we now have at GE is, to me, the magical formula.

I love learning. When I stop learning it's time for me to leave. Arriving at GE has inundated me with learnings about the technology behind power, healthcare and aviation. These fields underpin the basic functioning of every modern society and we tend to take them for granted, but understanding how electricity is generated, how it's made cleaner and more affordable, and how digitisation can be harnessed in this space is exciting for me.

Having the good fortune to be married to a medical doctor has given me insight into the public and private healthcare space, so to be working for a company that produces machines that save lives is fascinating.

The third reason I was drawn to the GE role was that I have always wanted to feel like I am being of service to my country. Born to public servants – my mother a teacher and school principal throughout her working life and my father having various roles as government health inspector, minister of the Gazankulu parliament and director of state-owned entities – I have always wanted to align my work with a greater purpose. Though GE operates in the private sector, the business is oriented towards building a world that works, in partnership with the public sector. In most countries, infrastructure for healthcare, power and aviation is the responsibility of the government, but in developing countries like South Africa the private sector is more involved in delivering services.

GE has an enablement mandate to find creative ways to serve the greater good as a development partner of the government. No economies survive without a healthy labour force. This is dependent on equipment we install in public hospitals. Every business requires electrical power to ensure that the country is competitive globally and attracts investment.

I find the work I do today is intertwined with the success of South Africa. We provide the infrastructure that underpins the president's Economic Reconstruction and Recovery Plan, just as GE is connected to the growth of all the economies in which it is present.

Some may ask why I remain in the private sector, rather than more directly working towards the public good from within the government. Of course, it is something I would love to do because it is unfair to leave this responsibility to others while we sit back and enjoy the benefits, but I am wary of the toxic and challenging environment. I know many people who have moved from private to public sector roles with good intentions and who have had their fingers burnt by politics. A good friend from my MBA group and a highly skilled professional, Dan Marokane, is an example, moving to Eskom as a senior director and group executive committee member, yet he suffered reputational damage as a result of baseless accusations and a lack of support. Though Dan was vindicated by the Commission on State Capture, it took him a long time to bounce back professionally from the setback. Vuyani Jarana, my erstwhile counterpart at Vodacom – head of the enterprise business while I led the consumer division – was equally unhappy as CEO of SAA and resigned after just 18 months.

A raft of similar stories causes professionals to be fearful, and to search for viable ways of being of service from a distance.

GE was a brand I could not ignore. It is undoubtedly one of the world's most iconic businesses and one of the US's most important companies, responsible for a third of the energy generated worldwide. The timing of their approach also coincided with great challenges I wanted to take on: the world is going through an energy transition, experiencing decarbonisation, climate change and sustainability concerns. To be part of finding solutions to these challenges is the stuff of legacy. It is already a legendary business, but has the chance to build even further upon its status by making the world a better place through reducing emissions, improving healthcare and rethinking the aviation industry.

Now in my second year with GE, I can reflect on the immense opportunity given to me and assess my achievements.

I am excited by the company's purpose, which is rising to the challenge of building a world that works. GE is responsible for more than a third of all electricity generated in the world. More than 90 per cent of all global power stations contain GE equipment, and over 80 per cent of the world's electrical distribution grids are controlled or driven by GE products and services. Whether from nuclear, gas, hydro, wind or solar PV sources, we provide end-to-end power solutions the world needs.

That more than half of the millions of people still without electricity in the world live in Africa motivates me to create breakthrough solutions to meet that need. As we South Africans beset by load shedding know all too well, electricity is the foundation of modern progress: it powers the light by which we study, the computers through which we communicate with the rest of the world, the base stations that carry telecommunications signals to keep us connected.

At the same time, electricity is one of the world's largest contributors to environmentally harmful emissions. Especially since the COP26 summit in Glasgow, Scotland, at the end of 2021, the world is looking for cleaner electricity generation that does away with fossil fuels. South Africa is by far the largest emitter on the continent, with more than 80 per cent of our electricity powered by fossil fuels. This is a once-in-a-lifetime opportunity, in which I am integrally involved, to find answers that do not exist yet.

GE is also one of the world's largest manufacturers of healthcare equipment, supplying products and services that are used to run hospitals. During the COVID-19 pandemic, the inequitable distribution of vaccines and medical technology – never mind doctors – became crucial in protecting the right to life in many poorer countries. This has pushed GE to find ways to provide care remotely, without doctors, through mobile and affordable healthcare solutions. Again, this is an unprecedented and exciting time of finding new ways to save lives.

The company's aviation segment was under the most severe pressure when I joined. GE has a 70 per cent share in the commercial jet engine market, as well as a significant share in the military market, where our equipment can be used to save lives in conflict situations. COVID-19 decimated international leisure and business travel, affecting the economic prospects of businesses that depend on connections with foreign territories. There is a great deal of uncertainty about how the market will respond when borders reopen – will people go back to travelling as they did? How many airlines will still be required to meet the demand for international travel? What equipment, refurbishment, service and maintenance requirements will remain?

This is another great challenge that excites me and stretches my personal capacity. To join a company that operates in three industries facing unprecedented change and requiring innovation is again taking me out of my comfort zone and resulting in a deluge of new learnings for me.

My experience at GE is confirming my belief that global changes driven by digitisation, technology and AI – accelerated by the pandemic – will reprioritise jobs and skills to favour the generalist. Those with multiple skill sets in commercial, technical, marketing and finance roles, those who have applied these across several industries and particularly those who have worked internationally will be best placed to sustain their work and employment in the face of change. Being able to plug into different geographies and industries will become vital as the fortunes of various sectors grow and wane.

I am fortunate to have built a career that maintains my relevance to business and keeps me wanted. I can be a marketer, a strategist, a general manager. I can work in Africa, Europe, anywhere – I have global mobility. I have experience in real estate, healthcare, energy, financial services, telecommunications, consumer goods and more. The single-company career model can still work – examples are Sim Tshabalala, Standard Bank Group CEO, and Shameel Joosub, Vodacom CEO. Both are highly successful and specialised, but in the future I believe it will pay to hedge one's bets a lot more and be open to a diversity of opportunities.

Another reason for me to feel fortunate to have this opportunity at GE is that the business is going through internal change. There are certain events that occur rarely for business leaders, but that will serve you well because of the accelerated learning they provide: corporate action, such as mergers and acquisitions, or going public via an initial public offering, or setting up a new business and brand. These are all very special events and bring to mind my experience with Brandhouse many years ago.

Trends toward digitisation and renewable energy signal a major shift in how most companies will operate – where they operate, how they generate funding, their key input ingredients. This is happening on a massive scale for GE right now, and it is a special experience for me.

This company is 130 years old and is going through a phase of transformation. For the first time in its history, the group will separate into three publicly listed entities, a shift that will be complete by 2024. Each standalone entity, as yet unnamed, will be the first or second player in its industry and will benefit from faster decision making, direct access to resources and a more targeted shareholder base. Going forward, management will be able to extract greater value from more agile businesses, and investors will be able to focus their investments and avoid the dilution of exposure to unrelated business interests.

I am a member of the separation committee, leading the activities in Southern Africa and deciding which entities should be formed and how the company should manage its communications about the exercise, and ensuring that we don't take our eye off our core business activities or lose market share while we're separating. The process has its detractors, who are uncomfortable with so radical a change, but I expect future results will validate the decision. I am already encouraged by the opportunities it will give our employees to specialise and the clarity it will provide to investors. This is a milestone project, and I am excited to be involved.

In terms of highlights during my time with GE, the strengthening of our relationship with the South African government through public–private partnerships in trying to find a solution to load shedding has been gratifying. GE was called upon by the minister and director-general of the Department of Public Enterprises to explore potential solutions. This was not a procurement call, but the strength of the relationship was displayed when we were asked to become a strategic partner, given our history of working with Eskom and private-sector customers as well as the group's experience in the rest of the world.

GE has maintained a clean record, unsullied by allegations of state capture, despite being significant contributors to major infrastructure projects such as Medupi and Kusile. The call from the government proves that our ethical and sustainable approach to business is a source of pride.

I also led a collaboration with the National Business Initiative, with research provided by BCG, to help guide South Africa's just transition to a net-zero emissions economy. I was part of a thirty-plus collective of CEOs tasked with assessing the potential economic and social impact of the green transition, meeting on a regular basis as an advisory board for a project team working on recommendations regarding costs and execution of the just transition.

I am very proud of this work, which the Presidency used as the basis of South Africa's representations to COP26. The outcome was nearly $9 billion of green funding to back the country's green transition, including the repurposing of power stations and new funding models to recapitalise Eskom as the country changes its energy mix.

Similarly, GE has engaged with the South African Department of Health to drive thought leadership on the National Health Insurance scheme, given our global healthcare experience. The real challenge for South Africa is the funding model and the scheme's affordability. GE is bringing breakthrough technology to market. We invested R77 million in a showcase clinic to demonstrate how the NHI can divert hospital visits to well-equipped clinics run by nurses.

Many hospital visits can actually be taken care of at a primary level, but clinics need the right facilities and level of competency. On behalf of the American Chamber of Commerce in South Africa, I led a delegation presenting to the parliamentary portfolio committee our views on the NHI and what is needed to make it work. We have also worked with the private sector on the model to address what is a dire need in the public health sector – more than 80 per cent of South Africans do not have medical insurance.

Since South African Airways came out of business rescue, we have also been working closely with the board and management on their future plans, providing creative solutions that will allow the airline to re-fleet and become fit for purpose in a changed aviation sector without breaking the bank.

To be a partner again in redesigning a business of importance is rewarding. These partnerships have resulted in a strong pipeline of orders and services from GE, which is driving improved results for the group in Sub-Saharan Africa. I have now been involved for two sets of results and each has improved upon the prior year. Going forward, I am confident that our inspired and engaged team will thrive.

As I said earlier, what really matters in business is results. It's the same as in sport – people remember the winners, the goal-scorers. We work in an ecosystem, and big projects teach you a lot about formulating alliances that are collaborative and provide wins for all parties.

Every experience of talking with my counterparts and peers is enriching. We have to understand their business fully to help ensure its long-term viability and sustainability.

In my role since May 2021 as chair of the U.S.–South Africa Business Council, which aims to expand the countries' bilateral relationship to drive inclusive growth, I meet with American executives interested in doing business in South Africa and we discuss geopolitical issues. I also get to interact with the US government, both in Washington and through the embassy teams to drive US investment in South Africa and influence enabling policies in both the US and South Africa. I am really pleased with the positive impact that partnering with the US Chamber of Commerce and the American Chamber of Commerce in South Africa (AMCHAM) – where I also serve as board member – is having in growing US–South African trade relations. This level of insight into global business trends has been nothing short of amazing for my personal growth as a business leader.

I have also taken significant strides in the area of personal reputation and brand management – what you might call thought leadership. I did not take this seriously in the past, but reached the point where my position in dealing with complex and critical issues for society, business and government necessitated a more public persona. People now expect to hear my thoughts and opinions on a variety of issues through public platforms, and I have embraced the responsibility – after a bit of nudging from those around me. After previously paying little attention to certain platforms, I have become an active LinkedIn publisher, sharing my thinking on impactful, innovative leadership. This platform is a great way to get immediate feedback and engage with my network, though it demands a thick skin when reading responses.

I have also enjoyed opening up to more guest speaking opportunities – particularly at business schools, where I love the intellectual vigour of engagements with students. It is an honour to receive a growing number of invitations to such conversations and I believe they add value for the students and for me, through the extensive preparation I do before speaking. These events – including interviews by journalists and podcasters – also allow for feedback and viewership statistics that can help guide my future thinking and topics. I am encouraged by the positive ratings and engagement statistics from my interviews thus far. Thought leadership and policy influence is critical to our work at GE, as it is key to creating conditions for market access.

Dealing with interviews has required me to improve my media engagement skills and preparation. One example was being invited to a conversation with Zimbabwe's minister of finance, the very learned Professor Mthuli Ncube. I had to prepare thoroughly, using budget speeches, strategy documents and even YouTube videos to ensure I was not out of my depth.

All this has added to my body of learning, but one of the greatest lessons in my GE role has been watching Larry Culp go about his work. He is a tough, focused leader – very demanding, but also laid back. He is strong-willed and clear without being overbearing, and promotes transparency, humility and consistency. This all sounds simple, but in action it is powerful and was a massive culture change for the business.

Like Larry, I have brought an external, customer-oriented lens to what we do at GE. Larry's typical leadership engagement event includes external guest speakers – particularly those who have led successful corporate turnarounds. There is never any question who is in charge with Larry at the helm, but he freely allows others to share what they have done to increase our organisational learning. Larry's primary achievement has been to identify where GE adds value and to be a champion of practical leadership. Through this approach, GE has demonstrated how and where it is making a difference in the world.

In all, I have never learnt so much in the space of a year. Larry's application of lean business concepts has simplified our processes and improved our problem-solving ability. Every day we strive for opportunities to make things better than they were yesterday. This continuous improvement ethic is vital in a large organisation because large corporates become overly complex, growing layers of red tape, raising artificial barriers and forgetting about the customers we serve.

It goes without saying that joining GE on 1 May 2020 created a few artificial barriers of its own. I have spent 95 per cent of my GE career dealing with my team virtually. I haven't even shaken hands with most of my colleagues. Despite this challenge, I feel like we have built relationships. It is not easy coming in as a leader and trying to take charge without ever actually meeting anyone. I remembered a piece of advice I received many years ago: 'Before you feel sorry for yourself, think of your neighbour and what they may be going through.'

I was able to look around for inspiration. Within my team, I was not the only person wanting to build relationships. I was also able to meet with many more people through digital platforms – and much more quickly – than I would have been able to do physically. At the touch of a button I was able to speak with GE leaders and counterparts from around the world, without being constrained by travel itineraries. My meetings with government officials became similarly streamlined, without the requirements of signing in, security and travel. The pandemic forced a rethink not only of my orientation as CEO, but also of the structure of the organisation.

What I was able to achieve in this regard in just one year I rate as one of my finest successes. While I cannot discuss financial performance on account of listing requirements, I can say GE globally is on a positive trajectory and investor sentiment reflects that.

One of my mandates on arrival was to drive transformation through GE in South Africa and improve our BEE rating and localisation of supply. This was an important task, since the company needed to demonstrate its commitment to the long-term prosperity and sustainability of the country.

The intent behind BEE is sustainability: the development of businesses, jobs, skills and preferential procurement is congruent with building the capacity of the country for a sustainable future. With such a young population, it is obvious that the establishment and growth of SMEs will drive economic inclusion.

After five years of being stuck at Level 4 contributor status, with the support of my team and the broader business, I managed to move GE to Level 1 in just 12 months. The lesson here is that a business need not work at incremental improvements, if your will and focus are strong enough. More importantly, for GE it means that within one year we have been set up for commercial opportunities that rightly require Level 1 or Level 2 status to participate, and which simultaneously position us to make a difference to the country's transformation agenda.

GE will be a significant player in the country's clean energy transition, safe return to flight and implementation of the National Health Insurance scheme. To improve capacity and delivery in all three of these fields, GE must have the right credentials and partners locally.

I love being the source of teachings and best practice, and we have demonstrated what is possible in a hybrid solution. Commercial wins like these are important and exciting, and rank alongside similar wins in healthcare. Our healthcare business, particularly in serving the public sector, is now significantly ahead of our plans – and I believe this is just the beginning for GE. The country's ailing health infrastructure is ripe for our services and solutions, especially in laying the groundwork for the rollout of the NHI. We strongly believe in our primary care capabilities, so much so that we are building a clinic in Mpumalanga to showcase them. Launching this clinic with the MEC for Health in March 2021 was a great illustration of what GE can do when our businesses come together. Our Power business donated the clinic from the CSI budget, and the healthcare team equipped it with state-of-the-art equipment, working in partnership with civil society. We are pleased about the jobs created and skills developed – and about the support of local business in the realisation of the project, worth nearly R70 million.

GE is also a strong leader in aviation in South Africa, and will help to resuscitate a sector that was grounded during the pandemic – as well as the associated tourism and hospitality industries, which are heavily dependent on air travel. We are actively involved in plans to reform SAA, partly out of social responsibility in ensuring that the airline becomes stronger and more sustainable. We also have a strong partnership with regional airlines, including private ones like the Comair group, Safair and Airlink. It's encouraging to see more and more airlines return to flight safely, and many estimating a return to pre-pandemic volumes earlier than previously thought.

I am also proud of the capacity we have built in GE's teams – especially through our graduate and internship programmes. GE awards hundreds of bursaries per year, developing and training talent. I am excited about our Future Engineers project, launched with the GE Foundation, which saw Johannesburg included in 25 cities selected globally to receive over R100 million in investment for improving access to science, technology, engineering and mathematics (STEM) skills for people from underprivileged backgrounds.

Our advocacy and bid were strong, and Johannesburg will now be one of 4 pilot cities for the programme's launch, determining best practice for how the other 21 cities will roll out their initiatives. It is a great honour that we will be assisting high school and university students from rural and underprivileged communities that lack STEM teaching facilities to receive resources, teachers and infrastructure – everything that will be needed to begin producing engineers.

In a country that needs so much more local innovation and more breakthroughs, this is an important programme.

GE has also exported talent into global markets. Just as I did at UBL, I love it when people leave to work with the world's best and return stronger, more prepared to take on bigger roles. It not only showcases South Africa's talent, but builds our business capacity.

At GE I have been able to drive change while learning a great deal. We are trying to solve incredibly complex problems to which the world does not yet have solutions, which is motivating. We collaborate across business departments and with external stakeholders to find solutions.

The world needs to decarbonise, and South Africa's economic ecosystem is currently tied to coal-powered electricity generation. This will require a significant change, which must come at an affordable price. The associated cost, job creation and technologies leveraged are all presently under discussion.

Similarly, healthcare facilities that deliver quality care are expensive to build and operate, particularly for rural communities, which means driving access to healthcare services will almost certainly include a component of remote diagnosis and artificial intelligence.

Searching for answers – such as how to bring healthcare costs within everyone's reach – is incredibly exciting and brings me into contact with a vast array of stakeholders. We are challenging ourselves to be innovative and inventive in a way that goes beyond what I have experienced before – even in telecommunications.

We are not merely looking to expand on existing concepts, but to make step changes in service delivery. If we do not bring a disruptive approach to the centre of GE's business, we may not have a sustainable business. This is a scary but exciting proposition, and we are notching up victories. GE recently announced the development of new technology that will reduce aviation fuel consumption by 20 per cent – the equivalent of removing 17 million cars from the world's roads. This is a significant move towards decarbonisation.

Our work on mobile health scanners, and wind turbine recycling and disposal, holds similar potential to improve the world's environmental stewardship.

As I look forward, this is the position in which I find myself – and I couldn't be happier. The world needs what GE does and will require our expertise in tackling crises in energy transition, coping with the pandemic and international travel. Seeing so many professionals working tirelessly through a commitment to finding solutions makes me proud and excited about the future.

Aside from the results, I am excited and proud to be delivering work that will leave a significant societal impact. I hope that one day I can look back and say I spent my career making a difference, in the bigger agenda. That is what drives me.

9

GROW YOURSELF

Studying for a four-year degree – particularly when we are young – cannot possibly sustain our work journey for the next 40 years. During our working life the world will change more rapidly, which requires us to engage in continual learning to stay relevant and competent.

Reflecting on my first 25 years of working, there are many skills I still need to hone. I was trained in business management, focusing on marketing and industrial psychology as majors, but my academic training was almost immediately supplemented by on-the-job training through the P&G Graduate Management Training Programme in sales management.

My technical skills in the art of selling came from modules like Persuasive Selling Format, which emphasises preparation as the groundwork for making a sale. I thoroughly enjoyed training topics such as managing sales calls, stock counting, order recommendations and closing a sale.

As I became more experienced, I began to learn about channel and key account management, along with further sales-related material. My training as an employee grew even more exciting when I attended the P&G sales college courses at the global commercial training centre in Brussels.

Training on the job was a key decision driver for me when I chose P&G for the start of my career. I knew already that a university qualification was important, but also generic. To fit in and perform within a business, one really needs customised training for that environment. This is why corporates invest in bespoke training, which is co-developed with a faculty from a major educational institution but enhanced by practical application. Companies like Unilever and P&G are world-renowned for their robust training programmes that accelerate the development of young leaders. For me, P&G had the added advantage of being new to South Africa, so I felt I would be working with senior leaders who would grow me as fast as the business was playing catch-up in its markets.

It also meant that more senior opportunities would open up as the company grew. The downside risk was that P&G would fail to entrench itself in its target consumer markets, become impatient and withdraw, but I was not deterred because there will always be an element of risk on the path to success and it is often true that higher rewards are accompanied by greater risks.

Over the following years I developed a keen interest in general management as a route to my goal, but this required me to develop my skills in finance, supply chain management, operations, and regulatory and public sector engagements, among others – even if I did not need to learn them to practitioner's level. These were skills I did not learn at university but which would ultimately become crucial to remaining relevant as I climbed the corporate ladder.

To illustrate, Amazon and Facebook did not exist when I was at university. In today's business environment, no business leader can survive and remain relevant without understanding online as a sales channel, the data and analytics that are generated from it, the technology upon which it depends and management of the direct customer relationships it entails.

Another notable trend is the massive growth in importance of corporate purpose and sustainability. CEOs need to understand the interchange between government, business and society in detail. When I studied for my MBA I remember an elective course titled Business, Government and Society, which was just one quarter long.

Today, a business leader needs to be conversant with the UN Global Compact and the Paris Resolution as a functional baseline. No business will survive into the future without topics like carbon neutrality and organisational purpose as standing issues on the executive committee's agenda.

These examples are a reminder to all of us that what got us to where we are today may not be enough to take us to tomorrow. We may even need to unlearn certain concepts and challenge our own beliefs as our surroundings change.

The way to do this is to grow ourselves through ongoing learning. The first of many important self-growth events that shifted my trajectory occurred soon after I had joined P&G. We were frequently reminded that each of us was responsible for our own development, rather than the company or the line manager. We were told to take charge of our own growth, determine our own career vision and identify the developmental areas we needed to address to get us there. This was part of a culture of being demanding of ourselves, since we were best placed to know what we were passionate about and the strengths we could leverage in achieving our goals. In this system, the line manager and company were resources in support of the developmental agenda – there to work in partnership with us through consultation and analysis. Then, it was up to us to work hard.

There were two leadership behaviours at P&G that really inspired me. The first was ownership, which amounted to taking accountability for our actions and mistakes and treating business assets as though they were our own. The second was initiative and follow-through – to see something through to the logical conclusion. This was intended to develop people who were action-oriented and could execute.

These two principles were to be engraved upon my career. When I joined Diageo there was a set of leadership standards and behaviours we were required to demonstrate and by which we would be measured. My favourite of these was Grow Yourself – a challenge to leaders to consciously locate themselves on a never-ending journey to improvement. Throughout my career, I have maintained the attitude that my actions will be purposefully and intentionally aimed toward self-growth. I owned performance review discussions and always walked in extremely well prepared to drive the agenda in a way that would identify areas for further development.

I was so demanding and uncompromising that I resolved to attend courses at my own expense if a company was not prepared to send me on training. My father had often said that what you learn nobody can take away from you. Investing in education and training is not just for the benefit of the company. It would be churlish to pass up an opportunity to take such a gift.

It became clear early on at P&G that I didn't have a solid foundation in finance. A single-semester course in accounting and another in financial management as part of my postgraduate diploma in marketing management was not enough to manage my region as a sales representative. If I were to grow into broader leadership roles I would not have been able to cope – let alone to become a CEO, whose core responsibility is the financial well-being of the company. In 1998, just two years into my career, I registered with UNISA for a year-long certificate in financial management. This was the beginning of a series of enrolments for various courses in financial and non-financial management while I was at P&G and Diageo. I took an interest in financial reports, befriended financial managers and asked many questions.

If the odds were stacked against me in moving from a non-financial background to a CEO role – or even a role in which I needed to report to people who spoke that 'language' – I knew I had to develop my ability. When I studied for my MBA in 2002, I took a few finance electives and even after I was appointed to my first CEO role I spent a disproportionate amount of time with my CFO to get up to speed on managing financial aspects of the business, dealing with auditors and so on.

Joining the board of a private equity company in more recent years was yet another step towards understanding and managing mergers and acquisitions, financial leverage and growing asset values to obtain a decent exit price. In this role, I am now at the heart of financial management.

As I have said elsewhere in this book, I believe in throwing myself into the deep end where I am forced to learn – mostly by doing. However, this does not happen without taking an active approach to learning.

Over time, I saw that to become a CEO I needed to appreciate the business as a system: I needed to grow beyond a functional leader in the area of marketing and sales, where my strengths lay, to become a general manager who leveraged various functions to make the entire business ecosystem operate smoothly. To move from where I was to where I wanted to be, I needed to complete an MBA. Since many of the courses were electives, I was able to stack my syllabus in alignment with my career and learning objectives.

I had been cynical about the MBA qualification because I had seen many people enrol for the purpose of obtaining the qualification and greater earning power without materially improving their performance in the workplace. In fact, I still believe that the inconsistency of performance among MBA graduates and varying standards of the qualification itself are damaging to the reputation of the MBA.

While I was hesitant to join their ranks, I knew the whole could be greater than the sum of the parts, considering the general management aspect. I also liked the future-oriented thinking, which was intended to prepare leaders to lead through novel situations. The opportunity to learn about other functions with teaching augmented by peer-to-peer learning was the clincher.

As it turned out, my MBA experience was powerful because I landed up in a class with some incredibly sharp minds from all walks of life – from academics to social scientists and entrepreneurs. For me, it was a great aggregator and morale booster to be competing with peers I thought were smarter than I was.

It also taught me that self-doubt can be extremely destructive. I emerged from my MBA more self-confident and assured, after somehow bungling my Graduate Management Admission Test, being rejected initially and having to negotiate to get into the course. I wrote representations and even met with the dean until I was admitted on probation. Ultimately, I finished in the top 10 per cent of my cohort, confirming that it pays to believe in yourself and not what others think you may be. I have done this repeatedly through my career, making the victories all the sweeter.

One of the highlights of my MBA was achieving a first-class pass for my dissertation on a research subject which was foreign to me – the road logistics industry. My research partner, Philip Kruger, and I interviewed more than fifty companies' owners, drivers, administrators and relevant government officials, completed secondary research, observed operations and more. Again, this was throwing myself into the deep end because I knew that if I wanted to be a CEO, there was a very good chance I would need to understand supply chain management, logistics, exports and imports, distribution, warehousing, inventory and more.

While these events speak to my willingness to take risks and learn, another discipline that has benefitted me in terms of personal growth is that of being coached and training as a coach. This is very closely linked with mentorship, which has had a tremendous impact on my career. Today, I am a qualified executive coach with corporate clients – senior leaders whom I assist independently on their growth journeys. I first attended coaching training in 2001 via a two-day programme in Cameroon, through Diageo, and subsequently attended further programmes.

During the Diageo Management Development Programme in Cameroon I first met one of my personal icons and future mentors, Gerald Mahinda, who at the time was financial director of UBL before becoming MD for Africa, the Middle East, Turkey and Pakistan at Kellogg. Gerald and I were among a handful of other attendees who were each allocated a coach while at the same time being trained to coach. The idea was that we could head back to our respective organisations and coach our own employees and peers. So began my experience with the value of having authentic, challenging conversations about leadership with another person.

A good coach can effectively place a mirror in front of you and reflect what you really are versus what you believe yourself to be. Done well, this can be a powerful exercise in unleashing your potential and enabling you to reach solutions by yourself, rather than being told what to do.

My belief is that we are often better than we know, and that the problems or issues we face today are not new – we have overcome similar challenges in the past. Engaging in tough and honest facilitated conversations with a coach can allow us to step back and see a situation for what it is, while coming up with a solution. This can be empowering because the solutions are ownable – we got there ourselves.

When I reached London with Diageo, I was identified as a high-performing, high-potential star within the business and I was hunting for promotion. When I went for a readiness assessment with YSC Consulting, I was judged not to be ready for promotion. Despite feeling deflated and disappointed, I used the opportunity to target the areas in which I needed to improve to become ready. I looked for a coach and Charles Mead from YSC stood out for me, so we began facing my 'demons' together. The alarming thing about such coaching for initiates is that it demands true vulnerability – facing the weaknesses and derailers we usually cover up with outward displays of confidence.

Having an honest conversation with someone who is there not to judge you but to help you unleashes a different kind of growth. If you know you have an ongoing relationship, with meetings scheduled once a month, it is impossible to fake progress between sessions.

Good coaches leave you with reflection points or 'homework' for action during the month. We have all attended training where, the moment we finish the evaluation form and leave the venue to return to our desks, we simply fall back into being the person we were. Coaching is not supposed to be a box-ticking exercise; it is intended to demonstrably change behaviour in execution. I often think about how I do things differently on a Monday as a result of training. Even if I change one thing about how I lead or conduct myself, I have gained. As your coach gets to know you better, it also leads to a greater responsibility to implement changes and show progress.

While coaching can be relatively general in approach, mentorship entails learning from someone who has more experience and a history of excellence in the area in which you would like to grow. People like Gerald, and Ekwunife Okoli, were highly successful CEOs and I wanted to emulate them, so who better to guide me?

Though I have ongoing relationships with various mentors, I also seek one-off sessions with others. When I became a non-executive board member for the first time I asked a mutual acquaintance to introduce me to Ralph Boëttger, a former CEO of Sappi and chair of several companies. Taking the initiative, I sat with Ralph and absorbed as many lessons as he could provide in our time together. My goal was to discover how board members and board chairs made the transition from being executives to dealing with CEOs at the other end of the table. How do you not stifle or micromanage another CEO, resolve conflict, deal with difficult situations?

I met with the father of a colleague, who had chaired various companies, because I could not say no to the opportunity to learn from people who had walked the path. That kind of learning is priceless and transcends any academic knowledge you may accumulate. I was able to ask the targeted questions that would help me achieve my goals.

I have done this many times in life – relying on people I admire to share their knowledge with me – and I have always been surprised by their generosity. I'll ask to have a drink once a board meeting is finished and learn from their experience, challenge my own thinking. I tend to be the youngest board member wherever I go, which means I get to learn from business founders and CEOs who have already contributed a great deal.

I also believe I need to give back: I am appointed to boards for a reason, so it cannot be that I use them as a learning opportunity without contributing meaningfully.

Sometimes it is enough to simply observe. At Vodacom I would sit back and watch Shameel handle the results presentations and investor conferences. I remember well the amount of preparation that went into such engagements. They form an important aspect of leading a business and cannot be taken for granted. You need to give it all you have, and that level of discipline and commitment – often over weekends and holidays – was part of good leadership.

In the modern context there are so many opportunities for self-teaching, even if we cannot gain immediate access to those with more experience. From management and leadership books to online video content and webinars, it is very easy to learn from a Fortune 500 company CEO being interviewed, presenting or answering questions.

If there's some aspect or skill in which you want to improve, you need to own the process. A soccer player listens to the coach who is on the sidelines because the coach has a different perspective on the game and is not focused on one player's role. This is enormously helpful in correcting errors, when extrapolated to the business environment. Find a coach, find a mentor and get the benefit of 360-degree feedback.

I am obsessive about embracing feedback from others and incorporating it into my self-growth. It is understandable that people want to avoid negative feedback, but it cannot be avoided through the course of a career and can be embraced to make us stronger. Consumers may not respond to promotions and advertisements, and products may fail to sell. These learnings allow us to take corrective action and improve. It is the same in the workplace, where cross-functional feedback from our peers, juniors and managers – as well as external suppliers – can provide us with a good sense of how we are performing, our capabilities and areas for improvement.

This should not be feared. I have learnt many ways of both seeking and giving feedback. The key is what you do with it. Generally, there is no shortage of feedback, formally and informally, and informal feedback can often be most authentic and immediate. The key lies in acting on it. I have discovered that if people see you acting on their feedback and improving, they tend to admire and respect you for it. Listening is an important skill, which is often underdeveloped.

Traditional corporate development plans and systems are usually designed to help you improve upon your weaknesses: we may be strong at five or six core skills of our job specification, but still be developing in two. A typical action plan would focus on those two skills, but I am glad to see that modernised development systems also recognise that we should also leverage our strengths to become better leaders. We grow faster by doing the things we're good at and like.

The things we don't like can be mitigated by action plans. For example, not every president may be a great orator like Barack Obama, but that doesn't mean they can't be highly effective. Instead, communication with the public or groups could be engineered to take the form of interviews rather than speeches.

Turning someone into an expert from a position of weakness may not be a realistic expectation, so the goal needs to be effectiveness. Similarly, a team should be constructed to deliver on certain outcomes, rather than placing the burden on one person.

I have found that performance management systems in corporates are underutilised. They may be commonly implemented, but their full capability and power are seldom harnessed. These systems tend to follow the same framework: agreeing on goals for the year, key performance indicators for measurement, and the specification of behaviours that must be demonstrated during delivery. There is usually space for personal growth goals to be listed, as well as support required to meet those goals.

Done well, this system can be very powerful in driving growth. As far as I am concerned, there is no grey area – the numbers and targets are there. As long as they are realistic but designed to stretch the person, consistent outperformance should lead to rewards and bonuses. If that happens for some years, the organisation cannot justify a failure to promote the person. Growth against a career vision is documented and does not even depend on the opinion of the line manager.

Where most people let themselves down is in using the performance management system as a tick-box exercise – not taking it seriously and not giving it the time and thought it deserves. This can be the fault of both employees and managers. Conversations need to be authentic, deep and serious, rather than rushed to meet a submission deadline.

I have used performance management systems to demonstrate what I want to do and where I want my career to go. I want to know what it will take for me to get my next opportunity for promotion. If someone is already in my desired role, I want to be able to model and mimic the right behaviour.

Some great advice I received early in my career was from a line manager who told me to always work a level or two above where you currently are. If you can do that, the business will realise you have outgrown your present role.

If you are a sales representative, how do you demonstrate that you can be a sales manager with reps reporting to you? What is it that the sales manager does that you can already start doing? This could be administration, presentations or account organisation.

A performance management system is, technically, an ideal feedback mechanism. Both you and your line manager need to agree on expectations, as does the line manager's manager. It involves building consensus so that there is no ambiguity about where you stand. It can be used for external opportunities, as can bonus letters, which are given to high performers.

Development is the most underutilised part of any performance management system. This is where an employee should indicate needs for coaching, training or other support to be more effective in a role. Take the opportunity to ask for support to avoid remaining static. There are usually funds available for skills development.

Development need not be seen as a corrective measure. It is not a sign of weakness to be trained; it is an acceleration measure. It gives you a chance to benchmark with a cohort of other delegates – sometimes internationally – and to learn skills that will benefit you in the long term.

Another benefit is that trainers are usually seniors in a business and they will take notice of those who perform. Training is seldom an innocent exercise and trainers usually are given a brief to identify talent. There are fewer roles the higher you move up the corporate pyramid, which means intensifying competition requires getting yourself noticed.

By the same token, some training carried out by third parties can be a thinly veiled money-making exercise and offer little value because it has been aggregated for as wide an audience as possible. My preference is to target knowledge I want and be trained by people who have demonstrated excellence in that area, or who are thought leaders in their field. I have attended many think-tank sessions hosted by consulting firms like McKinsey, Bain, Deloitte and Boston Consulting Group where clients are invited to topical discussions focusing on examples of businesses that are winning at a competency.

I have learnt to choose carefully and tend to favour highly customised seminars that drill down to a particular aspect of what I want to learn. Invariably, I have found myself interacting with peers from other industries who are dealing with similar issues and we are all able to interrogate success case studies. For my purposes, this has encompassed a range of topics from digitisation to leadership in the unique African context and agile work models.

Networking is an important facet of attending such conferences, but cannot be for the sake of it. Again, a highly aggregated and broad event is unlikely to yield many useful connections; a more strategic and focused event is much more likely to lead to follow-ups. I have met several business partners at events we have attended out of a common interest and vision.

One interesting variation of this concept was the Deloitte CEO Retreat, which brought together key clients, executives and their partners for weekends away. We could discuss topical issues with key decision-makers in the style of a public-private partnership, and indeed one of the weekends featured the president of South Africa as well as the premier of Gauteng, among other representatives from several government departments.

These events were designed to create insights and stimulate debate in a relaxed environment, and I found it enlightening and powerful. Bringing leaders together can often avoid a waste of effort: many solutions to problems have already been found, and few problems are genuinely unique. We can simply improve upon and customise solutions to meet our needs, which we can only learn if we network with our peers.

Lifelong learning requires taking an active interest in personal development and being prepared to be vulnerable about the things we don't yet know. As a leader, I need to keep learning about where the world is headed and the trends that may affect my business. I encourage anyone with leadership ambitions to make time to learn regularly and to seize every opportunity to improve. Be deliberate and intentional about your personal and professional growth.

Learning enough about something to become a trainer opens up a whole new level of knowledge, because everyone you teach will ask different questions and challenge you in new ways. We work not in isolation but in ecosystems, so it pays to know as much about the cross-functional value chain and our part in it as we can.

After completing my MBA I joined Milpark Business School as a lecturer. I began lecturing in marketing, but was soon asked whether I could take on an operations management course. Though I was no expert, I agreed and forced myself to learn it thoroughly at the risk of being embarrassed or evaluated poorly. This was part of my development by doing, and foreshadowed my role with GE.

GE is a heavy industrial goods business, manufacturing jet engines and medical technology, building power stations and engaging in heavy engineering. I'm no engineer, but a year into leading teams in these industries I know a lot more about them because the only way to be effective was to throw myself into the deep end and allow myself to be a fast learner.

I even completed an Advanced Management Programme course through INSEAD Business School at the end of November 2021. Learning never stops.

10

GROW OTHERS

My career growth was accelerated by observing four key characteristics of skilled leaders who served as great role models for uplifting others.

First, I believe every leader who thrives and succeeds tends to surround himself or herself with a great team. This is easier said than done, since every company competes for talent and, even within an organisation, line managers compete for the internal superstars. I have adapted for my own use a strict yet supportive approach to managing talent and performance.

Securing the best team and getting them to work well with each other is analogous to assembling a soccer team. The team will never deliver results if its superstars cannot work well together, which means the primary task of the manager is to take an interest in the dynamics of interpersonal relationships.

A mistake many leaders make is to leave the talent and people performance management task to the human resource department. What they don't realise is that their own performance is heavily dependent on the performance of the team around them. It baffles me that some leaders either suppress their people or surround themselves with weak performers so that they remain the smartest people in the room. This leader archetype is called 'The Diminisher' by Greg McKeown and Liz Wiseman in their book, *Multipliers: How the Best Leaders Make Everyone Smarter*. I strive to be a multiplier leader, often hiring people I believed were smarter than I was, and whom I believed carried greater potential than I did to lead bigger businesses and even multinationals.

I acknowledge that my responsibility is to create a working environment and culture where such talent can thrive and win. I believe strongly in the adage that people don't leave companies; they leave line managers.

At UBL, I was not happy with the balance in the team I inherited – the lack of diversity in skill and thinking made me feel I required an astute operator to drive our strategy. This may seem like a contradiction – an operations expert to drive strategy – but my issue with many strategists in the marketplace is that they lack operations experience and approach their task from a consulting background.

Consultants can bring a wealth of experience from different industries and countries to a large organisation, including analytics tools and hundreds of real-life case studies that we can use as best practice for problems we encounter. They can also provide great frameworks for thinking about and understanding complexity, management of stakeholders and delivering persuasive presentations to influence executives. However, an absence of hands-on experience that has delivered business results for a sustained period to create shareholder value makes the consultant approach problematic. They don't usually have insight into the politics of the organisation, or a well-rounded picture of what happens at every stratum of the business – partly because executives sometimes wish to conceal the reality of operational failings or project execution risk.

This is particularly true in business reorganisation projects, operating model optimisation or cost-cutting exercises, where conflicting information may be withheld. To mitigate this, consulting firms usually hire retired C-suite executives as senior advisors, to obtain a practitioner's view of client issues and insight into the inner workings of organisations.

I took this route when I recruited Juliana Kagwa to join UBL as strategy and key accounts director. Juliana had been country managing director for Heineken in Uganda. UBL was the second-largest brewer in the country, with about 43 per cent market share compared with SAB's 50 per cent. Heineken was a distant third – a new entrant, but growing quickly by making inroads into the premium end of the market. At the time UBL enjoyed a 70 per cent share in the premium beer market and similar levels in premium spirits, but I admired the way Heineken was executing – and, indeed, they are world-renowned for punching above their weight in this respect.

Within a year of my arrival in Uganda I knew I wanted to have Juliana in my team. I learnt that Heineken had recruited her from Diageo with a promotion to a position for which she had known ambition. I was also told that Diageo counteroffered, but failed to keep her. Nonetheless, I was undaunted because I was intent on bringing new life to UBL – the kind of energy the market had not seen in a long time.

UBL had turned around, our confidence was rising and our market visibility was increasing, along with market share. We were gaining external recognition as an employer of choice and as supplier of the year. Even within Diageo we were winning accolades. Our people were in demand globally – in 2014 UBL sent more Ugandans to Diageo jobs abroad than in the previous five years combined.

I supported these moves to showcase the talent we had in Uganda, as well as to demonstrate the pipeline and depth that countered popular perceptions of Africa. It also served to create a succession pipeline for proudly Ugandan future executives. True to my intentions, most have returned to the country and UBL, where they continue to drive the business.

My goal was to get Juliana to fix our key accounts, even though she did not come from a sales background. In the new role I created, I wanted her to bring new thinking to our strategy as a beer-dominated business. I tasked Juliana with 'premiumisation' of our mainstream execution, to outsmart innovative competitors like Heineken. More importantly, I wanted Juliana to leverage her knowledge of the premium and super-premium beer segments to convert drinkers to our international premium spirits business. I knew the high-end, elite customers of Kampala loved Juliana, her work and its impact. She had direct market experience as she and her husband also owned a popular high-end bar in the city.

I did not have anyone on my team with such an end-to-end understanding of the market landscape and track record of successful execution. Juliana also understood UBL very well, having worked for the business for more than ten years from graduate level. An important learning from bringing Juliana back to UBL was that it can be extremely beneficial for talent to leave, learn new things and then return – more highly skilled, stronger and with broader perspective.

Personally, I had experienced similar growth after spending two years outside Diageo from 2006 to 2008, running the Nando's franchise business. It made me a much stronger leader and the entrepreneurial flair of my work contributed to the acceleration of my career after 2008.

I knew I needed to have a career conversation with Juliana to reach clarity about her end goals and ambitions. We discussed her personal purpose and I had to convince both myself and her that a return to UBL would help her achieve those goals. Ultimately, my reasoning proved to be sound, the move was successful, and Juliana delivered excellent work, having been promoted twice since her return.

Similarly, in 2017, while I was at Vodacom, I replaced the executive business manager of my team – also known as the chief of staff in my office – with new, young talent. The role was originally designed and specified for a senior leader with ten years of experience, preferably in a telco and across multiple functions. However, I elected to hire a very young former McKinsey consultant who had worked for a mere two years since graduating and was on secondment as a brand manager at a leading beverage company.

What swayed me to hire Zweli Mfundisi was that we had met once for dinner and talked. I was blown away by his intellect, level of thinking and irreverence. I knew then that, as my chief of staff and the person responsible for preparing my strategy documents, town hall presentations, monthly reports, board packs and so on, Zweli would bring a fresh perspective and thinking that did not align with my own.

Another factor working in his favour was that he was 25, born in a digital-native era. I had not studied business science, did not excel at quantitative subjects, and had not been trained by one of the world's leading consulting firms into a new framework of thinking.

Zweli was essentially the photographic negative of my skillset, my opposite, a junior and someone who would challenge me to learn and be inspired. He did incredibly well, related excellently with me and the team, and brought a new sense of deliberate, conscious visibility to the work we were doing. No wonder I enjoyed his contributions for just 18 months before he was recruited to study an MBA at Stanford. He now runs a successful renewable energy business.

In similar fashion, I benefitted from people who sponsored me and took a risk on a youngster – starting in 1981 when I was casually following my mother to work but was drawn into school by her colleagues. They saw my potential when I participated in learning and insisted that I progress with kids who were older.

Later, I was offered a role in finance as a finance graduate trainee at P&G, without having studied in a financial stream at university. I was told I had the aptitude and attitude for finance, and that the company would provide the necessary training.

A few years later I was hired into a marketing manager role by Mike Joubert at Guinness UDV without any direct marketing experience, having spent five years in sales. Then, in 2013, I was promoted to a CEO role at UBL in my first country executive position, leading an experienced team of local and international executives without ever having been a functional director or executive committee member.

I built up a track record of success and excellence in the telecommunications industry, energy, healthcare, property and aviation without prior experience. All of these moves were – on the part of those who backed me – calculated but risky decisions. In each case, someone saw my potential and I dared not disappoint them.

For my part, I was bold enough and confident enough to accept these challenging postings, which helped develop my appetite for risk-taking. I respect experience but, by the same token, believe too much of it in the same environment can become a liability, creating blind spots, arrogance and a lack of agility.

I like taking a risk on talent. At UBL, in a quest to achieve greater business efficiency, synergies and focus, I decided to merge the corporate relations director role with the legal director role. I hired the then legal director, who had no direct experience in corporate affairs but was a highly competent and astute lawyer. While she was initially not convinced that the combined mandate could work, we had a career conversation similar to Juliana's and she accepted the challenge, going on to become one of the top corporate affairs professionals in the region and delivering world-class work.

The key was that I saw something in her – beyond what she saw in herself. I believe leaders must develop the ability to spot exceptional talent, and harness and grow it. At Guinness UDV I headhunted an internal employee from the sales department to move to marketing. Again, we had a conversation about why I thought the person would be great in the role, and how it could link to his career ambitions with my support. He moved to Cape Town to join my team.

I have long believed in marketing as a profit centre, not a cost centre. I wanted marketers to be more commercial and not beg for budget but deliver returns on investments made in brand building programmes. I found that marketers from commercial roles just 'got it' better and quicker than classically trained marketeers – many of whom could not read a balance sheet or income statement, let alone prepare a business case.

I was also surprised to find that many marketers shied away from post-project reviews as they could not quantify the benefits of the activity. Yet I believed – and still do – that one can demonstrate the value of marketing spend. In fact, it is easier to see the consequence of *not* investing in brand building.

My rationale behind employing an ex-sales manager to be my brand manager was premised on driving effective marketing, blending the classical marketing approach with a commercial marketing approach. To cut a long story short, he went on to become one of the most celebrated marketing professionals in South Africa, acting as marketing director of several businesses in consumer goods and financial services.

If you invest in growing people who are ambitious and have capacity beyond their current jobs, it can be a blessing to provide new assignments to watch them grow and reach their potential.

Many of my personal assistants went on to be successful in other roles. They credit me for providing the encouragement and space to take on assignments outside the scope of their day jobs. I provided project work to allow them to prove themselves, as well as supporting them through studies, where appropriate.

Jeanne Siebert, my first PA at Diageo, was an energetic person with an extremely positive attitude and, at 33, was ten years older than me. I quickly surmised that she had strong skills in finance and could offer more. Jeanne was ambitious but not impatient – comfortable in her role but hungry for running a portfolio.

Beyond being a PA, Jeanne could analyse reports, identify problems, give me input on what she thought was going on in the numbers. She also networked well and knew everything about what was happening at the company. Through work we did together, Jeanne moved on to an assistant role in finance and we stayed in touch even after she left the corporate world to run her own estate agency. With my encouragement and permission, Jeanne added more value to the organisation and has ultimately done well for herself. It was a proud moment for me to see her become an independent business owner.

The seeds for her development were sown in our career conversations: I listened to her ambitions and encouraged her talent. When Jeanne left she was replaced by Jeanette Harris, who was well educated and intellectually strong. It was clear from the outset that being a PA was an entry point for her.

Jeanette was much more interested in marketing and communications, and I would task her with press releases, PR statements and plans, where she provided an advisory voice I needed. Jeanette later moved to the Smirnoff Ice marketing team as an assistant brand manager and then went on to have a successful career as a brand manager.

When I got to Uganda, I was supported by a fantastic PA, Dorcus Kanyago, who was an incredibly strong performer. We had authentic conversations about her talents and where she wanted to go in her career. Dorcus was very proactive and a breath of fresh air; I don't like having to tell people what to do.

Dorcus took control and demystified my office – she was strict but accessible and she became a trusted advisor. My diary was perfectly arranged and everything happened when it needed to. I think Dorcus was not viewed so positively by my predecessor, but I gave her room to operate and constant feedback. She moved on to one of her dream jobs, as an HR manager – a job she is still doing today. I love spotting talent.

Not all my PAs have followed a similar arc, but I firmly believe that organisations are filled with people who can do more than their current roles allow if they are nurtured and inspired: PAs, cleaners, forklift drivers – those doing honest work and performing well in jobs they could find. We have a responsibility to help them grow, and to recognise capacity. When people are stretched and inspired, they perform at an elevated level.

Succession is extremely important to me and is the second impactful leadership trait I would like to unpack in this chapter. At Diageo I was trained to believe that a successful leader needs to have identified at least one 'ready now' successor for their role – someone who could take over immediately, if required to.

The foundation of my deep belief in open and transparent succession planning was built at P&G, which had a promotion-from-within policy. To this day, all P&G global CEOs and senior leaders come through internal promotions. Every line manager had a responsibility to grow their people and was actively measured on their teams' success.

The question was always (perhaps a bit crudely) put thus: 'What if you were hit by a bus tomorrow?' From a business continuity and risk mitigation point of view, you needed to develop someone who could do your job. More positively, I took this to mean that, if one of my team members could comfortably do my job, then I could rest properly while on leave. If my team members can handle most parts of my work, that frees me up to work at an even higher level – on more innovative and strategic work that would allow me to push the envelope of the business and deliver transformative results, rather than being bogged down in daily minutiae. By working at this higher level, because I have trained and empowered my team to manage minimum deliverables, I get to set myself apart and deliver higher levels of work that get me noticed – accelerating my own growth.

Even better, and most importantly, the business feels comfortable promoting me or moving me to another role where I can grow and thrive, knowing that I have not left a vacuum in my previous role.

In my team, talent management conversations are very serious and aim for either progress if the team member is happy and thriving, or an exit if they're not shaping up.

As leaders, we must be prepared to have great and uplifting conversations about people development, promotions and growth, but also to engage in the tough conversations about exiting talent where people are not living up to their promises despite interventions. I have experienced difficult situations where, by mutual agreement, we have terminated employment of people I considered friends but were mismatched in terms of expectations about performance or organisational culture. I have asked people to leave an organisation, only for them to thank me later because they realised they were at the wrong place at the wrong time.

For some, this was the wake-up call they needed to pull themselves together, restart in a new environment and go on to deliver exceptional results. If such conversations were avoided, some of these individuals would have run the risk of disappearing into performance oblivion through complacency and a lack of authentic performance appraisals. My training as an executive coach has proven helpful here, helping me to handle awkward conversations in a balanced and constructive way.

I am proud of Alvin Mbugua, my former CFO at UBL. I marvelled at Alvin's intellect, communication skill and sheer charisma whenever we interacted. We spoke about his career ambitions and he was very clear about wanting to become CEO of a business. He was encouraged to assume a market CFO role first, to gain commercial experience, and it so happened that my CFO had reached the end of his assignment following a promotion to a bigger role within the group. I wanted Alvin in the role but was unsure about the fit for many reasons – including the size of the challenge in Uganda and his capability at the time.

After a few meetings and discussions about his career path and how I could support him, we embarked on a partnership with Alvin as CFO. I was particularly interested in having a finance head who would enable the strategy, unlock commercial opportunities and be expansive in thinking to drive growth and grow the top line rather than just save our way to margin enhancement.

Alvin was that and more. I have no doubt that my success at UBL was due in part to our partnership. I mention my pride because, just as we intended in our partnership, he went on to become CEO of UBL and did a fantastic job – and was then promoted to the role of MD of Diageo Caribbean and Central America.

Similarly, Mariam Cassim, one of my direct reports whom I had coached and worked with for two years, was promoted to a group executive committee role at Vodacom towards the end of my time with the company. This was a proud moment for me. Mariam continues to shine and deliver great results. We still enjoy a mentorship and friendship today.

I also look with pride upon great talent like Khensani Nobanda, group marketing and corporate affairs executive at Nedbank, who worked with me twice in different organisations during her career, as well as Nhlanhla Mbhele, chief executive: brand at Sanlam, who was a brand manager reporting to me years ago at Diageo. I headhunted Abey Mokgwatsane from the role of CEO at Ogilvy South Africa to join Vodacom as brand director, on the promise to help with his development and career growth. I supported him with mentoring even after my days at Vodacom, including helping to get him to the Saïd Business School at Oxford for his MBA. I was very pleased when he was appointed chief marketing officer at Investec Group, where he is also a member of the executive team.

The current marketing and innovation director at Diageo Uganda, Emmy Hashakimana, as well as Mark Kivuma, who holds the same role in Tanzania, were both my protégés during my time in the country. Then, there are successful entrepreneurs like Mdu Ngcobo and Jeff Madibeng who, like their corporate counterparts, credit me with contributions to their career growth and expanded perspective.

I love seeing people grow and reach their potential. Many people have told me I challenged them to reach heights they did not think possible. I tend to believe more in my people's potential than they do, partly through the belief that we use only a portion of our total brain capacity. Mostly, what we're doing when we're 'thinking' is really just retrieving and recalling information. Every day presents us with challenges for which we could tap into our brain power, and therein lies more intelligence than most people realise. I've seen it in myself – giving up on a challenge or problem because I'm too lazy to think. When I sit down and push myself to think about it and apply my mind properly, I'm often surprised by the solutions and breakthroughs that emerge. I believe we have to afford ourselves time and space to think problems through.

I challenge people at work, in my social environment and even my children to come back with a new approach or solution, and the results are uniformly surprising. It was this approach that caused me to embark on a formal journey as an executive coach. I had benefitted from being coached and realised that the coaching relationships during my career had all been transformational. How could I not want to impart this knowledge and benefit to others?

Coaching is the third important external component of career development that has driven my personal growth. When I signed myself up at GIBS to take part in an executive coaching programme in 2019, I wanted the formal certificate, but I also wanted to benchmark myself against the latest thinking in coaching. I liked that this course was accredited by the International Coaching Federation (ICF) and that I would meet with other coaches to understand the practical side of the craft in greater depth.

I had completed various coaching courses in the past – mostly corporate. I had trained in different approaches and methodologies, and all had in common the ethos of not providing answers directly and using feedback as an important part of the coaching conversation. This was a skill I was able to apply in my career as a line manager.

At the GIBS course, I was a member of a diverse group of about twenty candidates from varying industries and backgrounds who sought formal training and recognition. This richness of experience contributed to rigorous debates and learning. Coaching is an evolving field, which meant that everyone had a different view on the measurement of effectiveness and standardisation.

I loved the use of technology in recording and playback of coaching sessions, role play and observation. I was fortunate that Vodacom had started an alumni coaching programme for senior leaders. The coaching was carried out by former Vodacom executives who had the cultural and operational context while also being qualified coaches. This convergence of skills was highly impactful.

A coaching relationship needs to be permeated by trust. I have coached more than a dozen Vodacom executives, along with other clients externally, to earn and retain my licence. The beauty of being in the service of others is that I grow myself simultaneously. I enjoy the reciprocity and instant feedback.

As chairman of a private equity investee company, Gammatek, I have coached the CEO and the CFO, mostly one on one, but I frequently find myself in a coaching role on boards through conversations and meetings that provide a non-threatening way for board members to obtain feedback, share challenges and discuss vulnerabilities.

Another platform I have used to impart knowledge is leadership events, which can take various forms. The latest is a chapter I contributed to *The Book Every Leader Needs to Read*, published by Tracey McDonald in 2021. I was asked by the publisher to base my contribution on lessons I had learnt in the workplace that could fast-track readers' development, as they would not have to make the same mistakes I have made. I'm pleased that platforms like this are democratising learning. The messages I wrote for the book are the same messages I would usually impart to mentees, but now the audience is that much larger and readers need not know me personally or find space in my diary to benefit from my experiences.

Similarly, I have found LinkedIn to be a great platform for sharing knowledge and helping to build the careers of others. I began publishing as recently as 2020, but I am glad I started on this journey based on the viewership and engagement statistics. The content seems to be appreciated and people take the time to follow up and engage with me. They also challenge what I say, which can be constructive for both parties. In general, I try to avoid overloading people with information, so I stick to a schedule of an article every six to eight weeks, but some of the more popular pieces have been updated on an ongoing basis and ultimately became chapters in this book. Maintaining this kind of interaction, and building on it, can provide a useful testing ground for concepts.

I have tackled various topics on LinkedIn, from taking a sabbatical to taking a CEO role and the Japanese concept of *kintsugi* – seeking not perfection but rather the opportunity to make something better through addressing flaws. This post had its genesis in an invitation to address a UCT MBA class and speak about setbacks and failures – a highly enjoyable interaction that made me realise more people than the MBA cohort would benefit from the presentation. I rewrote it as a LinkedIn article.

I have similarly expanded my reach through webinars as a panellist, participating in global conversations in real time with a much wider audience than would be possible at a physical event. Over the years I have found myself participating on a lot of panels and have become highly selective about virtual engagements because the preparation can be demanding of time. However, both immediate feedback and subsequent viewership metrics can tell you a lot about improving your content and craft so that you continue to grow as you try to grow others.

That said, physical conferences still matter. If I'm invited to be an anchor or facilitator, I enjoy the preparation. A good example is an International Law Association event held in Uganda to discuss ways in which lawyers could enable faster economic growth on the African continent by reducing red tape. I was asked to deliver a keynote address and facilitate the conversation, which was a great opportunity to share learnings with some top legal minds. What I could teach was the experience of working directly in digital, because I was with Vodacom at the time, while trying to learn as much as possible about their language and views on development.

I also really enjoy being invited by non-competing firms to speak at leadership and management events to cross-pollinate ideas without having to worry about confidentiality. For example, in my current role at GE, I was invited to speak on innovation by Liberty.

In a much more direct manner, mentorship allows me to act as an advisor – sharing knowledge, skills, pitfalls and experience with someone in a similar position. Usually, mentors are older or more experienced in a particular field and provide words of wisdom. I am often approached by junior members of an organisation who seek help for challenges particular to our industry, business and role.

This takes time, but there are several channels through which to pursue it. I participated in formal mentoring programmes during corporate courses, such as at Vodacom, where we'd be allocated mentees. I assisted a customer operations director from Vodafone Qatar and a sales region director from Vodafone India over periods of six months and, as is usually the case, my mentees would ask for extensions so that we could stay connected after the end of the formal arrangements.

I enjoy mentorship because I love imparting knowledge and guiding people towards solutions. There is an intellectual challenge inherent in the arrangement. You are required to place a mirror in front of the mentee, be open to communication and help them learn from your mistakes.

I have engaged in mentorship throughout my career, even on an informal basis when people reach out to me for help. This can be a one-off event, given time constraints, but it can be very effective. When I was running five Nando's franchises as a co-investor, and now as a franchisee for AutoZone, I use mentorship as a way to drive performance of the leadership team in businesses where I am not operationally involved.

By the same token, mentoring also needs to work for the mentor. I would not engage in mentoring if it didn't make me learn and grow through a trade exchange. For example, Vodacom is full of highly technically skilled people, who over time would love to expand their horizons into commercial or general management. This was a great combination for me.

Through my activities at YPO, chairing an Ethos company and dealing with entrepreneurs, I have been able to mentor business founders on how to sell their ideas to corporates and influence people in a corporate organisation. At the same time, I was interested in their mentality: the agility, picking up ideas and scaling up quickly to make something from nothing. I learnt how to operate a lean business and improve efficiency.

The fourth characteristic of good leadership that can transform the fortunes of an organisation is a focus on graduates and management trainee programmes.

I have always been a fan of working with graduates because this is how I got my start in the corporate world. At companies like P&G, given their promotion-from-within policy, I have seen graduates grow to become CEOs. The key is the grooming of potential.

Earlier in this chapter I spoke of talent spotting – it is obviously beyond the scope of a business leader to be involved in graduate recruitment, but a business should be structured to maintain a consistent influx of fresh talent from tertiary institutions. In 1997, one year into working at P&G, I was appointed to lead recruitment at UCT because the company wanted someone still relevant to university networks. I was a campus head, tasked with recruiting the next cohort of graduates, liaising with the career office, and speaking at graduate recruitment events and guest lectures to targeted faculties.

As I have mentioned elsewhere, P&G's driving ethos was that 80 per cent of our time should be spent building the business and 20 per cent on building the organisation. This was in the service of sustainability and building organisational capacity.

Graduate trainees are not burdened by legacy ideas and bring with them the latest thinking. At the same time, they absorb knowledge and can respond very quickly and in surprising ways if you provide them with space to be innovative.

It should be no surprise that some of the world's largest corporates, like Microsoft and Facebook, were started by graduates who were not limited by legacy approaches, approvals or red tape.

I love the naiveté of graduates, the speed at which they work, the innocence of their grand ideas. With appropriate guidance, they can make things happen. During my career I have coached and mentored many graduates – some of whom have gone on to fill very big roles, making a difference at large organisations. This has been very gratifying for me.

When I was at Diageo, our graduate scheme in the UK brought in youngsters from various universities and I replicated the setup when I returned to South Africa, establishing relationships with tertiary institutions – especially the engineering faculties. We had been struggling to attract engineers and talent from Johannesburg, to which we had relocated a significant number of our operations. Diageo needed engineers to handle the technical aspects of brewing, process design, efficiency improvement and equipment maintenance – not to mention to be involved in finding new ways to blend ingredients.

Diageo was up against competitors who were more entrenched in universities as employers of choice, such as Coca-Cola, Unilever and Johnson & Johnson. Not many graduates around Johannesburg knew about Diageo or the opportunities on offer. Since I was working with lifestyle brands, we'd do activations, host production facility tours, offer vacation jobs as promoters and brand ambassadors, and position ourselves as a 'cool' employer. That landed us a lot of graduates. Then we worked on an internal system to ensure that the support structure for graduate entrants was in place.

I liked that Diageo's method was to start all graduate trainees in a commercial, customer-facing role to ensure that they learnt the heartbeat of the organisation – the operational side of the business and being in service of the customer. Then they would rotate into other areas of specialisation.

In Uganda, the exercise added a great deal of value. Collaboration with universities helped them produce better-prepared graduates who were work-ready. The institutions came to understand the demands of our work in a real environment and – through UBL's ongoing feedback – could compare levels of graduate preparedness against competitors.

The funding arrangement for graduate schemes is an important component. At Vodacom our graduate intake was substantial, and I was appointed as the executive sponsor for the programme. It had previously been run by the HR department, but I strongly believed it needed to be more integrated to be more relevant to our value chain.

Vodacom needed to be deliberate about this integration in the face of a high attrition rate and a lack of advancement from graduate level. As sponsor I advised on some changes that would help retain graduate talent, and we subsequently hosted the annual Vodafone graduate event that saw graduates working on projects in a simulated incubator and was later adjudged to be a tremendous success. We achieved some amazing results – because the organisation placed a greater focus on talent support and development in a real operational environment.

We also introduced a youth executive committee, realising that, in the tech space, Vodacom was competing with companies run by young people. When we visited Silicon Valley we met technological innovators and entrepreneurs in their twenties and thirties, shaking things up, changing the world.

In Africa, where the average age of the population is 19 and only 3 per cent are older than 60, there is a gap in insight into the lives and challenges of young people. If the market we were serving was young, we needed to start leveraging ideas from our younger employees. The youth exco featured employees in their twenties who competed for their roles and were coached by the real exco. The result was a massive shift in the way we thought about how we should do business, while inspiring our younger employees to take responsibility and ownership of the business.

I have continued with that mentality at GE – a business that sponsors more than two hundred people every year through bursaries. From that investment we draw future talent, future engineers, future leaders. It also keeps us fresh and relevant.

If harnessed correctly, graduate programmes can ensure the sustainability of an organisation and provide real jobs for employees – even if they are interns. More often than not, we are surprised by what we can learn from them.

11

THE IMPORTANCE OF PHYSICAL AND MENTAL WELL-BEING

As executives, our most important asset is our health. Much of the work we do may not be physical in nature, but it nevertheless requires us to be energetic, sharp and 'present'. When we are not feeling well, our productivity and decision making are compromised.

We've all seen it in the workplace: people struggling to stay focused and alert in meetings when they are tired, failing to make valuable contributions or perspectives during important discussions.

How many business leaders have suffered heart attacks, strokes or other devastating health failures because they led unhealthy lifestyles and didn't cultivate an appropriate work-life balance?

How is this relevant to my life and a book about my exploits in the business world? Many studies have shown that healthier and fitter people are more productive. The World Health Organization's 2021 World Health Statistics show that hypertension, obesity, physical inactivity, tobacco use and harmful alcohol consumption are among key risk factors underlying the growing incidence of non-communicable diseases worldwide. The WHO's report demonstrates that obesity among adults 18 and older, across all income groups, has been rising globally over the past few decades, with 650 million obese adults in 2016 – a 50 per cent rise since 2000. The report also shows that, on average, men consume three times the amount of alcohol consumed by women.

Healthier people tend to be more productive – they take less sick leave, they're more energetic at work and they stay mentally sharper for longer during the day. This all means healthier people can deliver more.

I have always believed in the ethos of healthy living, but I have not always practised good habits in taking care of myself. According to the book *The Secrets of CEOs* by Steve Tappin and Andrew Cave, as many as 75 per cent of business leaders admitted to not exercising regularly. Many blamed it on a lack of time and excessive travel but, really, these are just excuses.

Just about every hotel where a CEO might be put up during a business trip will have its own fitness centre. I have travelled extensively for work and know that, unlike the hotel bar or the buffet station, the hotel gym is one of the most underutilised facilities anywhere you might stay. Some even have swimming pools, but these are usually relatively under-utilised and you're unlikely to bump into any CEO jogging in the precinct around their accommodation.

A business leader can spend as much as a third of his or her time travelling and consequently eating at restaurants. While it is common practice for many organisations to insist on annual executive health checks using their contracted wellness organisations, as part of their risk management regime, we have all heard of share price crashes due to the CEO of a major organisation suddenly falling ill or dying unexpectedly.

I recall one large organisation I worked for reviewing the statistics of the annual health assessment of their top 100 executives: 75 per cent of those who drank alcohol consumed much more than the recommended weekly units for adults and there were at least twice the number of smokers than was the average for South Africans of their age group. In general, the executives were also overweight and unfit.

I resolved my own problems through moving to the UK, where I reignited my love for cycling in 2008. Until then I had been unfit for the first 11 years of my career. I was like many of my peers, who were provided with a gym benefit as part of our remuneration but hardly used it.

The move to the UK brought with it the enabler of convenience – I was irritated enough by the heavy traffic to start using public transport for my 10 km journey from Ealing to my office in Park Royal. This still took about half an hour in the morning, as opposed to 45 minutes by car and 40 minutes by train since there was no direct line. All options seemed excessive until I learnt that there were dedicated cycling lanes and that this method would get me to work in just 15 minutes.

Even better, the government would pay 50 per cent of the bicycle purchase price to incentivise the reduction of congestion and emissions, so my state-of-the-art bike cost me just £450. The balance of the actual £900 purchase price would be funded through monthly deductions from my employer over six months.

There was a massive drive in the UK towards a greener economy, such as the employer bike ownership scheme and congestion tax for driving your car in areas with heavy traffic or historically important areas the government wanted to protect. We were also allowed to drive our personal cars to the office for only four days out of every five-day work week. The fifth day was supposed to be a green day, where we would take public transport to the office or work from home.

I am highly attuned to financial incentives and I abhor inconvenience, so getting 50 per cent off the price of my bike while also finding the quickest way of getting to the office was already a double win for me – getting fit made cycling to work an extremely compelling proposition. I began cycling to work three days a week and I loved it.

Through Diageo's cycling community I met more self-propelled commuters within and without Diageo. Relationships are very important in a work environment, but they can be built or improved outside of the office. It is no coincidence that team dinners, off-site annual conferences, sports days, year-end parties and the like are so assiduously planned by companies. They create an environment outside of the office for people to get to know each other and bond.

Trust is developed when people get to know each other genuinely, when they come to understand each other better. People become more open to sharing and collaborating when they trust each other.

Any organisation's leader will tell you that executives sometimes make decisions on the golf course, a restaurant or a bar, rather than at their desks. We should not underestimate the impact of familiarity and comfort on team performance.

For me, cycling to work was not only convenient and financially beneficial; it ended up giving me access to other cyclists with whom I could cultivate enduring relationships.

I remember riding the famous Diageo annual cycling challenge, which takes place every year in Scotland. Scotland's terrain is mountainous and cold, so a 90 km cycle can be daunting. I was a commuting cyclist and hadn't trained for anything more taxing, but as a lover of challenges I signed up, thinking it would motivate me to improve my cycling.

After much deliberation about how we would get to Scotland, my wife and I decided to make a trip of it and drive the 650 km from London to Scotland in our small 2005 Vauxhall that we used for everyday running around. We also had to find space for our son, just a few months old and still breastfeeding.

What a trip. I had forgotten that in the weeks leading up to the event I needed to travel extensively through both Nigeria and Ghana. I barely found time to train. The night before the race we drove for nine hours through unexpectedly heavy traffic and heavy rainfall – all for the simple love of riding my bike.

The cycle itself was brutal. My sheer determination and forcefulness saw me through, but I resolved somewhere around the umpteenth bend in Scotland that I ought to become more serious about my fitness. I decided to train more and do cross-training to achieve more holistic fitness.

Of course, this all fits with my character – I soon added running to my routine. Like cycling, which I'd done during my primary school years and then stopped, I used to run the 100-metre races at both primary and high school. I was a sprinter, with a certain amount of agility allied with my small frame, which made me nippy. I could accelerate quickly and I loved getting to the finish line first over such a short distance.

I think my love for sprinting is the twin of my experience in the family business, which made me extremely competitive and determined to succeed. Reuniting with running was exciting, but in the absence of that competitive thrill I had to find a way to get my adrenaline pumping.

True to my style I quickly registered to run the Oxford half-marathon in 2009, alongside my wife. I had never run a competitive half-marathon; the distance challenged me, being twice my usual 10 km. I knew this would get me working. Registering my wife, who was far fitter than I was, in the same race meant there was no way to back out – I needed someone who would keep me true to my commitment.

Again, running the half-marathon was tough. We walked the last two kilometres but celebrated that we'd finished before the three-hour cut-off time – by two minutes, if I'm not mistaken. Considering that Mosima now comfortably achieves times below two hours for 21 km and I consistently run around 2:10, it shows the power of simply deciding to get started. It provides a base from which to measure our progress.

Over the years, due to commitment to training and encouraging each other, we have seen great improvements. Again, running helped my integration into the UK Diageo office because I became a member of the company running club with my colleagues. We had a training programme at the office gym on the treadmill, as well as regular park runs. Bonds and friendships were formed, which led to meeting up socially outside work time, like barbeques at each other's houses.

I was aware that it improved our team performance. As colleagues we spoke more, related more and were united in doing something we all loved. Ironically, at Vodacom a few years later, one of my relationship highlights with group CEO Shameel Joosub was when we played soccer on the same team. He played as a midfielder and I as a striker, where we enjoyed a wonderful combination – his hard work in the midfield fed me great passes, which I was able to convert through my pace, positioning and accuracy.

Though I am less good at other areas of the game, like dribbling and heading, I played to my strengths and so did he. Together we delivered goals and it won the team many games. Initially, neither of us even knew that the other had a passion for soccer – it was only through extramural activity that we discovered another point of connection that improved our burgeoning relationship.

Running in the UK also led me to indulging in another passion of mine, which was raising funds for the underprivileged and providing assistance in line with my purpose. Following the Oxford half-marathon I'd found so gruelling, I decided to step up my training for subsequent races with the Diageo running club. It turned out that the club was also a fundraising team for the Diageo Africa Water for Life projects.

Through running we would raise funds for nominated causes in a country of our choice, as long as it was related to water preservation or purification to ensure that communities had access to clean water. This was a fulfilling mission: doing something we loved and was beneficial for ourselves while also making a difference to people who needed help.

I also signed up for the workplace gym, which made sense because there were personal trainers available to help us with fitness programmes. There was a community of morning trainers who came to work early, but through participating in organised events like weekend runs, rides and boot camps we also rubbed shoulders with executives who got to know us so much better than would have happened through formal business meetings.

Though I have a passion for soccer, I am not a great player – I am just an opportunistic goal scorer. While I was at UBL I discovered that the company had an employee soccer team. The team competed in the Ugandan corporate league against companies like Standard Bank, Nile Breweries, MTN, Unilever, Coca-Cola and Pepsi.

The UBL team fared well, regularly topping the 18-team league. Two of our players were great soccer players – Demola Adeyo, our sales director, and Shane Healy, the supply chain director. The team selected anyone who was good enough, so it spanned forklift drivers, cleaners, merchandisers and directors from the executive team. Titles and ranks were equalised, which meant it was a great bonding opportunity.

I love watching soccer, so I attended a lot of the games to support the team. Mostly, these were in the evenings and over weekends because the corporate league is for full- and part-time employees who are on duty during office hours. It seemed a big deal for the staff to see me in the stands because my predecessors did not attend, and neither did the CEOs of other companies.

I would arrive on any given Saturday with my kids to watch the UBL team; I wasn't always able to stay for the full 50 minutes, but I wanted to make sure the team saw me on the touchline, and I am told it meant the world to them. I think it is no surprise that our employee engagement and net promoter scores were almost instantly elevated on our path to eventually becoming an employer of choice in Uganda.

Sports break barriers. In South Africa we have seen how our racially divided country was united by the 1995 and 2019 Rugby World Cup wins, and by hosting the 2010 FIFA World Cup as well as the 1996 Africa Cup of Nations win. The feel-good factor and unity phenomenon can also exist in business and I believe it needs to be properly harnessed.

At UBL I was very impressed by the way employees took to various activities like yoga and using personal trainers, who came on Wednesdays. I'd find employees running, doing squats at the company bar and so on. This culture continued after my time in Uganda, with my successor Mark Ocitti leading a team of employees in a climb of Mount Kilimanjaro. The current CEO, Alvin Mbugua, is an avid marathon runner and recently led a Water for Life run from Kampala to Mbarara over several days in relay teams – a distance of 300 km.

One thing I miss about UBL is how we worked hard and achieved much in the office, but had a lot of fun together away from our desks. The old adage, 'Work hard, play hard,' allowed us to gel as a team because we all knew we had each other's backs.

There are many in corporate offices who are reluctant to participate in activities outside of the workplace with their colleagues – whether they see it as an extension of office politics, forced socialisation, sucking up to leaders or simply taking up time they could spend with their families. Some are also averse to activities they don't particularly enjoy. This dynamic can be present when executive teams of mostly white males – typical incumbents in South African corporate settings – suggest cycling, hiking or golf as team-bonding exercises. Such activities also have the baggage of perceived or real gender bias.

My experience is that, while it is true that some activities can be exclusionary and can be used to build parallel executive structures or political alignments, if done correctly they can instead be a force for good. The point is the development of trust. This is the key to team building. What really builds trust is knowing that you are aligned with your colleagues, and they have your back. The professional setting of the workplace is often not enough to inculcate such levels of trust, which will inevitably need to be built through other activities outside of work.

There are many ways to achieve this: annual team-building events, family days at work, Christmas parties, company off-site charity drives like painting schools or dropping off food parcels – the list is extensive. Something as simple as a team going out for a meal or eating together at the canteen can do wonders.

Shying away from these activities does not position an employee well, in my view. Relationships are critical, even externally. Customers want to know and trust you. So do investors, regulators and government bodies – these relationships all benefit from 'face time' and provide greater insights into the people you need to deal with. Socialising at work, even for those with introverted personalities, is an essential part of growing one's stature and impact in the workplace.

I am pleased to see that many businesses and executive training initiatives focus on physical and mental well-being and the importance of 'wholeness' at work. In 2013 I attended one of Diageo's most loved and highly rated executive development courses – the Diageo Leadership Development Programme, or DLPP for short. This is aimed at senior executives at Diageo – typically those from medium to large country offices of strategic future importance, referred to internally as priority markets.

The DLPP is *the* course to attend, since it is run directly by the global executive committee of Diageo, with some sessions facilitated by the global CEO. In our case, this was Ivan Menezes, who tended to stay for the full-week duration of the course. It was a privilege for us to spend the week with people who presided over one of the largest FMCG businesses in the world, learning from and sharing our perspectives with them. This happened especially between sessions.

While many of the topics were expected, such as company vision, strategy, leadership values, expected standards from leaders, organisational culture, personality assessment, the competitive environment and macro-issues facing the business, one topic that fascinated me was simply titled Energy Management. It was allocated almost half a day.

This session began with a questionnaire about how much we exercise, drink, smoke, go on holiday and other metrics. Then we engaged in deep discussions about our lifestyles and, surprisingly, even deeper discussions on issues like diet and rest. We openly unpacked the issue of work–life balance and the challenge of finding enough time in a day. It was enlightening to learn how little exercise most of us were getting. When we looked at the literature on these trends, we found there were many more executives in the same boat.

The major learning was that many executives work hard, but not necessarily effectively. We talked about the origins of lifestyle diseases which emanate from lack of sleep, excessive drinking, smoking, poor diet and lack of exercise. We even spoke about our weight.

Going back to Uganda after that, I started taking my diet seriously and hired a personal trainer, Michael, who was based at one of Kampala's top gyms. We met four mornings per week at 5 a.m. Under Mosima's guidance our helper Jan, who was also one of the best cooks I've ever met, prepared very healthy dishes.

I was five kg above my normal weight when I arrived in Kampala and I had to work hard to shed the excess. I enjoyed beginning every day at the gym because it gave me energy for the rest of the day. The sessions with Michael, while initially very difficult, challenged me to reach strength and fitness heights I didn't know I was capable of attaining. Seeing my weights for chest or leg presses, or simple arm exercises, grow month by month, and feeling my endurance and enjoyment improve, was a visceral reminder that even in our work with dedication and focus we can do things tomorrow that we thought impossible today.

While in Uganda I also took up golf. Again, I sought professional coaching from one of the country's best-known golf professionals, Deo Akope. He was incredibly patient at our biweekly 7 a.m. appointments. This was a later time slot than I would have liked, but we needed light to play and sunrise would not comply.

There are a surprising number of golf tournaments in Uganda, many sponsored by UBL through our various brands. I knew of many customers who loved the game, and so did some of the regulators from the tax authority, the treasury, as well as the agriculture and trade ministries. It became a great platform not only for stress release and enjoyment, but also meeting and building relationships with people.

My friends back in South Africa laughed at me and even mocked me because I had sworn never to play golf, thinking it a low-energy sport that took up too many hours. However, since I am purposeful about relationships and blending, given that most executives and politicians in Uganda played golf more than I had anticipated, I decided to learn how to play to gain access.

Discipline and boundaries are still important. I began to enjoy golf, but it does take an excessive amount of time and I decided to be intentional about planning and allocating my time for playing it. I limited my games to 18 holes per month, or two 9-hole rounds. I realised I could become addicted to chasing a handicap but was intent on simply becoming competent enough to play a few games without being embarrassed. Anything more would carve out too much of my time.

Importantly, I found another benefit to my recreational activities – time with my family. My son Nyiko took an interest in golf when he saw me going to play, wearing my gear and asking if he could accompany me. We ended up training together with Deo, bonding on the golf course. From not having enough father-and-son moments to finding an activity we could enjoy together helped relieve work stress and improve my productivity while also spending quality time with my son.

The effect of being more active was that I was less daunted by my workload. I found myself more relaxed even in tackling the most pressing and difficult of challenges. I was told I seemed more energetic and my perception was that I had greater clarity of mind. Away from the office, I was dreaming big, reflecting and talking with my peers, who were CEOs in banking, construction, aviation.

Suddenly I wasn't as lonely in my station – my problems were similar to those of my peers. If the relationship permits and there is no competitive conflict or confidentiality issue, one can get input and advice from external peers about navigating leadership challenges.

I found my physical activities so helpful and beneficial that when I returned to South Africa I continued with the same successful formula that had kept me sane in Uganda. I pay tribute to my personal trainer in Cape Town, who was also the physical trainer of a top Premier Soccer League club. He taught me the importance of body conditioning and stretching after exercise to avoid injury.

He was very strict about readying my muscles before embarking on heavy, strenuous weight-bearing exercises. In Johannesburg, Sbu at Dream Body Fitness in Sunninghill got me to lift the kinds of weights I never thought possible, focusing on building my lower-body strength. I didn't realise it at the time, but this became the foundation of my confidence and improved performance in cycling.

In the same way, Lincoln, my personal trainer at Virgin Active Waterfall, was an accomplished Comrades Marathon runner and pushed me to better my running. He made training fun, through his passion, jokes and the soccer fan rivalry we had – he is a staunch Kaizer Chiefs supporter while I am the same for Orlando Pirates. We had a great partnership and he introduced me to co-training out of necessity. I insisted on 5 a.m. slots but they were already taken by other clients, so he paired us up to share the time.

The resulting element of competition, not wanting to be outdone by the other trainee, made me raise my game and become fitter faster. I had originally been apprehensive about sharing the slot but was quickly reminded about the power of teamwork.

My trainer at Virgin Active Kyalami Corner, Fatima, taught me about working smarter by getting my technique right. She focused not only on the number of repetitions, sets, weights and speed, but also corrected and optimised my body stance, breathing and movements. I found myself, again, improving more rapidly and enjoying the workouts more.

Finally, Ananius, my current trainer, focuses on full-body training and incremental build-up of strength. He is very strict about avoiding injury and consistently reminds me that our bodies are much more capable than we think – handled correctly, they can surprise us by unleashing results when we've put in the right effort.

This has led to progressive boosts of confidence in my physical ability, time and again raising my levels of endurance and strength. We can do more than we think we can: most of us have barely scratched the surface of what we can achieve, physically, for one reason or another. This applies to exercise and sports in general – most often it is simply a change in mindset that can bring a breakthrough.

My trainer has often loaded up weights I found too heavy and I've given up. But then he may load the same weight again without telling me and I've been able to lift it because my brain wasn't blocking me. I have found analogous situations in work, where a suspension of current reality in one's mind is the best way to find new solutions and create new realities.

I also pay tribute to Charles, my boxing trainer, and Michael from Powerlab, who taught me most of what I know about cycling. I believe in doing things correctly rather than fumbling around and wasting time and energy in self-discovery. While there is ample space for self-discovery in most of what we do, it can be extremely inefficient. Why recreate the wheel if it already exists?

Rather, I rope in those who have the skills and can observe and understand what I'm trying to do in order to help me improve. This is one of my fundamental beliefs in innovation: there is no need to do something completely novel. Challenging yourself to improve on the points of friction in existing processes and activities can yield far greater returns.

This is the reason for calling attention to my many personal trainers and coaches. For those who can afford personal training, I recommend it. In just a 30-minute session, under professional guidance, it is possible to achieve much more than in a self-moderated one-hour sessions. If I attend four sessions per week I am saving eight hours – a full working day – per month through being more efficient.

What is an extra day worth? Suddenly, personal training doesn't look as expensive. As with everything in life, it's about prioritising the things that matter to you.

I begin most of my daily activities at 5 a.m. during the week, which provides me with an energy boost for the day. To start gym at this time, I am required to get out of bed at 4:15 a.m. after five or six hours of sleep. I tend to work for 11 to 12 hours a day to get home at 7 p.m. for dinner with my family or at a work dinner function.

I also exercise over weekends, mostly at my three-hour 75 km group rides on Saturdays, which begin at 6 a.m.. On Sundays I do recovery 10 km runs and, if there are no races that weekend, I will cycle again. It's a heavy schedule but it doesn't disturb my work and I mostly do these activities with my wife, which brings yet more quality time together, doing something we both love and care about.

More importantly, these activities are scheduled to maximise our time at work, rather than take time away from it. I wish I could work eight-hour days, but it is impossible – success in the workplace brings added responsibilities and demands on one's time, which leads to working harder.

Despite my regular running and cycling commitments, I engage in other activities to maintain diversity and keep things interesting. I have a low boredom threshold, so cross-training allows me to focus on different parts of the body while mixing up my activities. As I write this, I am back in Cape Town for a short family holiday – this morning we went hiking, surprisingly for my first time ever. We walked a 14 km trail along Table Mountain, which was fun. Now I have another activity to add to the list of things I enjoy.

My family and I love getting away on holiday to rest and recuperate. I learnt the importance of regular breaks while in Uganda, in my first role running a company and tasked with an urgent turnaround. Knowing that my time there would be hectic as a result of industry and internal company challenges, Diageo was aware that it would take its toll on us. As part of my package I was offered what is commonly known as an R&R allowance – rest and recuperation.

I recall using the first one to take the kids to New York. The second saw me take my wife to Cuba. Both were fantastic holiday destinations. My family and I subsequently visited Mauritius, Bali, Spain, Italy, Portugal, Kenya, Mozambique and the UK, among others. Similarly, we have travelled extensively within South Africa, enjoying the many wonderful domestic treasures this country has to offer. That said, we have more local destinations remaining on our list – in the Northern Cape and Free State in particular.

I am proud to be a citizen of a country with such abundant beauty, culture and heritage. Yes, we have our problems, but as an experienced traveller who has been exposed to a great range of countries, I can safely say ours is a gem with a great quality of life.

Many executives short-change themselves when it comes to holidays. What I have witnessed is that they are often not *present* even while on vacation – answering emails at the beach, working through the night while the kids are sleeping, not really taking the time to connect with their partners.

Sadly, given the gender imbalance at the top leadership level, it is the wives who shoulder the burden of taking the kids on excursions while their husbands work from the hotel. Worse, other executives do not take leave in an effort to artificially impress their bosses – displaying extra effort, commitment and sacrifice.

For me, taking real time off means switching off. Yes, it is irresponsible to turn off your phone and shut out your work life completely, because something disastrous may happen while you're away and most of us are safety and crisis officers as part of our roles – but taking real time off is critical for recharging and returning to work refreshed.

Taking some days which involve no real work at all will allow one to return to work more creative and productive. When we are unable to stop in such a fast-paced environment for a protracted period, we tire quickly and our domestic lives suffer.

It is often our home lives that end up donating time so that we can attend to work matters – how many executives miss their kids' sports days or school parent meetings, or cannot even drop their kids at school every morning? I am not surprised to read that more than 50 per cent of Fortune 500 company executives are on their second or third marriages.

Our spouses give a lot to support us in our journeys, yet our success can make them suffer. Drifting apart from our partners is not glamorous. A holiday where an executive is present and engaged with his or her family multiple times a year makes a lot of sense and is a chance to connect with the partners we have chosen and love.

For me, holidays also have a business-related upside: it is time to stress-test the reserves bench, to use a sports analogy. When executives take holidays they get to nominate identified successors as acting CEO to see if they are up to the task. One can observe the resilience and sufficiency of a team by letting them operate without their leader. Many executives have admitted that the COVID-19 pandemic and lack of direct supervision due to remote work arrangements have led to them discovering hidden stars in their teams. These are the people who rose to the occasion, delivering new solutions at previously unmatched pace in unprecedented situations. I have heard many of these stories, where leaders are amazed by the talents of team members they have known for some time but who suddenly emerged and delivered when it mattered.

Do we give our team members enough chances? Are we too often self-obsessed? Do we doubt that the business can function without us? Real empowerment of staff and delegation of work, including hiring people you think are better or more highly skilled than you are, is the sign of a great, confident and progressive leader.

In short, holidays are important. We work very hard, so equally we ought to allow ourselves time to play hard. We all need balance. The inevitable reality is that we face difficulty regularly in our private lives, which has the potential to affect our work and career success. Life happens – like everyone else, executives get hospitalised, have accidents, get injured, deal with wayward children, lose loved ones, get divorced, are scammed or make bad decisions.

As much as we wish to lead perfect lives, our circumstances are imperfect and we have to develop coping mechanisms. I believe one's spirituality and emotional balance are important and must be both protected and harnessed.

I can only imagine the kind of mental strength and fortitude that executives like Giovanni Ravazzotti and Sol Kerzner must have required when they stepped out of retirement to return to CEO positions after they had handed the baton to their sons, who both tragically passed away in separate aviation accidents. Not only did they have to deal with the loss of a child, but also needed to reassure investors of publicly listed companies Italtile and Sun International that the businesses would weather the leadership vacuum.

Similarly, Bob Collymore of Safaricom and Steve Jobs of Apple were just two of many executives who passed away while in office. I can only imagine trying to lead a business while in pain from cancer, as both of them described. When your capacity has been decimated by waning energy levels and medical treatment and you are uncertain of the time you have left, this must certainly be traumatic.

I have experienced personal trauma and have had to lead through it and I know it's not easy. Showing resilience through it can be the difference between making it to the top or not. One cannot afford to crumble.

Through these experiences I was helped by my beliefs. As a spiritual and religious person I have always had the support of my pastors in church, as well as fellow congregants who have prayed for me and with me. It helps that, as a family, we share the same beliefs. We would pray together – my wife, kids and mother would often join in prayer for us, even over the phone.

I also believe in counselling, so would seek help from professional counsellors, just to give me the space and tools to deal with the matter at hand. My coaches and mentors over the years have also helped me deal with challenges. Sometimes, as executives – and more so, as men – we bottle things up and try to deal with them ourselves, even as the issues weigh us down. This approach inevitably leads to the issue causing problems at work, where we can be judged negatively.

How can we shoulder massive responsibilities running big organisations with complex problems if we cannot organise our personal lives? I believe it is possible to find the time to counter the factors that cause stress in our lives – it just requires being creative. We cannot be optimally productive if we are under stress and strain from personal and family problems. For me, counselling, coaching, mentorship and prayer have proven very effective.

12
LEADING THROUGH IMPERFECTION

Since this book was written during the COVID-19 pandemic, lockdown restrictions and the business challenge of rebuilding, I felt it important to share my perspective on the unprecedented demands placed on leaders during this period.

My first thought is that the actions and decisions we made as a matter of routine in the lead-up to the year 2020 will certainly no longer be applicable or appropriate for a post-COVID-19 environment. At the same time, while we must adapt and find new ways of operating and new strategies for doing business sustainably, there are limits to what we know about the future. Executives and business leaders are currently encountering operating conditions for which we have not been trained. In a word, it is imperfection. I aim to inspire leaders to raise their game in the face of such stern challenges.

Getting to the top of the leadership ladder is not as difficult as it is made out to be. I believe most people deserve the leadership stations to which they aspire, and often lack guidance rather than talent.

I hope what I recount here will be of inspirational value, given that no two businesses are entirely alike. It is impossible for me to be prescriptive about how to deal with imperfection, but I will share some of my stories and the lessons I have learnt so that readers may interpret them and extract their own learnings for their circumstances.

Looking at my experience of the impact of COVID-19, I was lucky enough to be invited to give three talks and act as a facilitator of a panel discussion with the African Philanthropy Forum (APF). This organisation brings together philanthropists from around the continent with a view to inspiring more able Africans to give of their wealth to help reduce the dependency Africans have on outsiders.

We cannot rely only on leaders who are doing great things for underprivileged people worldwide, like Bill Gates, Bill and Hillary Clinton, Richard Branson and others who run donor NPOs. For real sustainability and contextualisation, we need more African dollar millionaires to give. The problems in Africa are so vast that international donors cannot solve them for us. In many cases, our governments are too poor in resources and their tax bases are insufficient to drive poverty eradication initiatives.

I have the honour of sitting on the advisory council of the APF, working with some of the most inspirational leaders I have encountered. At its annual conference in October 2020 I facilitated a discussion about giving during and after COVID-19, leveraging technology and the Fourth Industrial Revolution to exponentially increase the impact of spending. We were forced to think carefully and critically about the social issues COVID-19 has exacerbated in Africa, which provided valuable broader context for leading a business in a society that is plagued by socioeconomic inequalities.

The second invitation was from Professor Kurt April at the University of Cape Town. He invited me to lead a discussion with UCT's MBA students on leading through imperfection. The focus of my talk was on the restoration of the image of leadership, which has been tarnished in recent years in both the public and private sectors. The confidence of many executives has been crushed by such unprecedented and complex problems in an environment in which many people are sceptical about the capabilities of leaders.

The third event that rounded out my perspective of the impact of COVID-19 was an invitation by Professor Mazwe Majola's Worldwide Institute of Leadership and Development – an organisation which brings together entrepreneurs and CEOs – to deliver a talk on what leaders should be thinking about as they rebuild post-pandemic.

The first of my learnings from these engagements is that we, as leaders, need to change our perspectives on the talent agenda. The nature of the employee cohort that an organisation will require and hire going forward will be turned on its head. In many ways this is happening already. The way we work will be different in the future. For the past year we have seen employees sent home to work without direct physical supervision. For most organisations, this is already a radical departure from their established method of operation.

Nearly all South African employees have always worked under direct supervision and their managers are used to managing people they can monitor through the workday. What businesses are learning now is that no two employees are alike, and that accounting for these differences can lead to improved outcomes. Anecdotally, I have heard from friends, boards and my own businesses that they have been surprised by the emergence and flourishing of talent they did not previously recognise.

Some people have thrived under the new circumstances, preferring the freedom of working in their own homes and private spaces. A lot of new performers have also enjoyed being free from office politics. By the same token, those who liked talking, showmanship and doing little more than being social butterflies have been exposed because their outputs are now directly comparable.

Many organisations will continue to reveal the depth of talent they did not see previously, discovering that their workforce is more resilient than they imagined. The challenge for leaders will be to continue to harness and inspire that talent remotely. Nobody has the answer yet, but as leaders we need to share and compare learnings as fast as we can and read all available literature to maintain the momentum.

The other important development of distributed workforce arrangements is that the talent pool from which a business can draw is now global. I have a data scientist cousin who was approached by a large UK-based retailer just before COVID-19-related lockdown measures were put in place. The initial approach involved relocation to the UK, but after the retailer realised its data scientists could work effectively from home, the job offer was amended to be a remote position.

Suddenly, the dynamics behind access to talent have changed. If geographical barriers can be easily overcome, this is exciting for South Africa's skills shortages. The same challenge applies: how to manage, inspire and drive talent remotely.

Companies will need to overcome the challenges of a virtual environment in finding ways to extend a sense of belonging, team spirit and organisational culture across geographically diverse teams.

Allied with this challenge will be the necessary adaptation to changes in physical working space. CEOs need to lead debates about the change from office-based work models. Maintaining and even enhancing productivity in a digital environment should be relatively easy. One of the worst time wasters in organisations is meetings – especially unnecessarily long meetings. Elon Musk wrote about this recently, saying that business leaders should instead spend their time walking the floor. For necessary meetings, Zoom, Teams and other platforms provide the functionality required, but I know of few people who enjoy these engagements.

As a consequence, I have found that, where board meetings used to take full days, we are now getting through the agenda in half the time, giving us half the day back. Strategy meetings now also take half the time they ate up previously. There is also no need to travel to meetings, meaning scheduling can become much tighter. While this is the positive, there are negatives to the digital-first setup which will need to be countered. These include making up for swanky offices in prime locations, which used to be a differentiator in attracting top talent.

This advantage has been dealt a significant blow in a distributed work model and the businesses that can provide alternative compensation to the prestige of prime real estate will regain competitive advantage in hiring human resources.

I believe those organisations that move into international talent pools quickest will also come out ahead. Throwing the net wider will mean gaining access to the best of the best at their home prices, rather than paying a premium to move and resettle them in another country.

Another human resource challenge thrown up by the pandemic and its associated disruption is the value placed on functional expertise and experience in an industry and role. I've never been a big believer in the celebration of functional experience. I think it is important to grow within the ranks of a particular industry or job to the competence and mastery level – especially for some fields like being a pilot or a soldier. Experience has its role, but I think it is not the only thing required to be successful.

The reason I think experience alone is an overrated and overvalued virtue can be demonstrated by a couple of examples: the leaders of Uber, which has grown to become one of the world's largest transportation companies, did not come from a transportation background. Elon Musk did not have much experience in the motor industry, yet he has gone on to build Tesla to be one of the largest companies in the world by market capitalisation. The market value of Tesla is larger than the combined value of its six biggest competitors in the auto sector.

Mark Zuckerberg runs one of the largest media companies in the world without any media industry experience. Without labouring the point, the same can be said for the founders of Netflix.

This leads me to question the value of experience. The 'ignorance' that comes with a lack of experience can provide the magic that creates breakthroughs. Sometimes, knowing too much can be a liability because you can sink too deeply into your beliefs and experience and avoid disrupting yourself. If your experience is grounded in training drivers, will you adapt to a world where autonomous vehicles dominate?

Self-disruption is difficult, but necessary. We need to imagine how we might disrupt and 'attack' our business model as a competitor. Facebook employs people to do just that – to try to make its business model irrelevant. The best way to defend your business model is to try to make it irrelevant and then adapt.

This has implications for the people we hire. Do you hire the most qualified people? The most experienced? I studied marketing and psychology and the first job I was offered from a forward-thinking organisation was a position in a finance department. They said they'd train me, which I have to admire. I was blinded by my lack of experience, thinking I couldn't take the job, but that company believed more in mindset and attitude and I admire them for it.

Through my career I have worked in various functions, beginning in sales, moving into marketing and bringing a different way of driving success in marketing into the departments I managed. Then I went on to become a strategy manager despite never having worked on strategy before. I negotiated my way into it and threw myself into the deep end with a pragmatic approach.

I believe we should concentrate on the value someone can bring to a role or function and nothing else. Many experienced people add little to no value, while an inexperienced person can surprise through being motivated to succeed and repay your faith in their ability. It is attitude and speed of learning that determines success, rather than linear experience.

With access to information and tools being greater than ever before, there should be no more hard and fast rules about the number of years it takes to move from graduate to management role and to become a director. Skills and information can be learnt and obtained much faster these days, which means that someone with decades of experience who is stuck in outdated methods may be doing a poor job in a digitally enabled world.

Younger employees have grown up in a digitally enabled world and are likely to have skills older employees lack. The reality is that the incumbency factor means HR systems reward length of service and years of experience, even as the overly experienced person may be becoming irrelevant. The risk is that the business ends up paying more for an ineffective manager, rather than less for a much more effective one. A CEO needs to understand and cultivate the right blend of youthful, energetic generalists with experienced employees.

Adaptability, agility and flexibility will see leaders get ahead in their careers in a post-COVID-19 world. Those who can learn fast, think fast and implement fast will open up more opportunities.

Every leader and every business has been impacted by digital transformation and it will only accelerate. When we were all restricted to our homes under lockdown level 5, many people began to experiment with online retail to avoid visiting physical stores, which has been a transformative change in our business landscape. I heard a joke circulating, wherein the question was who really drove digital transformation at any company – the CEO, CFO, CIO or COVID. Of course, the punchline was COVID, but the humour was in the truth it carried. Many CEOs who would never have approved remote working arrangements were forced to set them up overnight, along with online trading capability.

Businesses that consider online to be a bolt-on have had a uniformly poor experience of it. There is no excuse in this environment – as leaders, we need to make sure we do online and digital well. The reality is that many business leaders are not trained for this. The speed of transformation requires us to apply our minds, humble ourselves and learn from people who understand the digital realm. My advice is to elevate the role of IT in an organisation. IT staff are not there to simply fulfil a helpdesk function – they have become a strategic product supply and development, customer journey development and cost-saving part of the organisation.

There are many complications that arise from operating online, such as protection of customer data, but leaders must take responsibility for data protection and cybersecurity. The damage caused by leaks and hacks of information at Absa and Experian show that the issue is important enough to be elevated to the top level. Customers will demand increasing levels of privacy, which may limit what organisations can do with data for engagement and customer targeting purposes. I expect this will become the next competitive battleground, which will require business leaders to have at least a working understanding of the technicalities.

Adapting to digital transformation is everyone's business, not just that of the CIO. It will require significant investment because doing it properly will mean investing not in parallel to other processes, but replacing them. I learnt at Vodacom and Boston Consulting Group that a business simply creates unnecessary complexity when it considers digital an additional channel rather than a new way of doing things.

Digitisation is an end-to-end journey and will require overcoming internal resistance. Behavioural change is difficult and takes time. Many leaders and employees think digitisation is far-fetched and will take time, and we need only look at the United States, where only 20 per cent of retail is online after 20 years of the technology being available – but the acceleration in digitisation is what matters. In one quarter, Amazon more than doubled its sales and employed an additional 400 000 people to cope with demand. COVID-19 is propelling the change even further.

Internal resistance can also come from people looking after their own power base. For example, the person who looks after property rentals at a retailer, whose job it is to open new physical retail space, could oppose a shift to digital to maintain relevance. How do we lead through change and bring people on the journey if the change threatens their employment? It will require being ahead of the curve in our own learnings.

Digitisation can create competitive advantage, such as deploying automated chatbot services for customer call centres. This comes with many benefits, such as better analytics about the customer experience. Similarly, technology can do away with the countless middlemen who simply take and relay orders for inventory, increasing efficiency and improving utilisation of warehouse space.

My view is that this change is akin to moving from handwriting to word processing on a computer. Those who show curiosity, learn faster and take advantage of the inevitable shift will grow faster in their careers. Learn as much as you can. Boards are increasingly looking for business leaders with digital and IT skills and experience.

The obvious caveat, however, is job losses. Digital transformation will have a social impact. I believe that, while the birth of new industries will create jobs in the long term, in the short term a lot of jobs will and must be shed. I remain positive about the long-term outcome, based partly on the number of people Big Tech firms like Google, Amazon and Facebook employ.

On a net basis, even though the new business models are disrupting old ones – such as in retail and the media – and causing job losses, there will be more growth. In South Africa, the challenge for leaders is that the economy is shrinking and is unlikely to recover any time soon. The country will continue to shed jobs for the next few years and leaders must make tough decisions about the sustainability of their operating models.

Job losses will bring personal strain and change lives, but without restructuring and embracing the future, the survival of businesses will be in jeopardy. Reconditioning a business to be sustainable should be recognised and celebrated. Shareholders look for businesses that can weather storms, which requires their leaders to demonstrate agility, resilience, tenacity and strategic depth for the repositioning.

It will require empathy. Observe the impact of restructuring at mining companies, which are so often centred on communities that are reliant on them. If you lay off 20 per cent of your staff, you can see the social and economic impact on the community. The balanced scorecard is there to help companies show connection, sensitivity and understanding, making it possible to give back through the development of small businesses, skills development and retraining, corporate social investment and social plans. Leaders who can demonstrate humility and humanity while making tough decisions to ensure sustainability of their organisations will be well placed to grow in their careers.

We will also need to understand not only the communities around our organisations, but also their buying habits and behaviour. Most businesses exist to serve the needs of an end user and understanding those consumers is critical to business success. If you satisfy their needs and create value in their lives, your business grows.

COVID-19 has disrupted lives to the extent that I doubt consumer habits will ever go back to what they were before. Consumers have made adjustments – seeking more value, trying to avoid wasteful spending and focusing on essentials. Uncertainty about the future has driven the concept of saving for a rainy day further into our collective psyche. As a result, luxury goods, travel and even education have been significantly affected. Job losses have seen subscriptions in private schools, such as those operated by Curro, drop through parents' financial defensiveness. I heard from the CEO of AutoTrader that searches for entry-level cars have grown exponentially, with most car owners downgrading their vehicles even in a low interest rate environment to save through greater fuel efficiency, lower running costs and reduced insurance instalments.

I foresee changes in the way people pay for goods (moving from cash to online and digital payment channels), take up medical aid, look after their health, consume alcohol and many more aspects.

The pandemic will affect many industries in unpredictable ways and the job of a business leader will be to discern the trends and position the business to be opportunistic: ward off threats and accelerate growth by staying one step ahead of consumers.

As long as you continue to be relevant to the needs of your customers, you will remain in business. I think all leaders will need to be conversant with technology, finance and the customer experience. Everything should be created with the customer in mind, which naturally calls for cross-functional teams and employees who are generalist in orientation.

This again speaks to the unnecessary premium on experience when we should be focused on leading more diverse, generalist teams. As leaders, we must constantly challenge the relevance of what we know. A good leader will need to change mindset regularly.

These examples prove the point: What does Apple do? The company may have begun with the Mac, but today more than 70 per cent of its profit comes from the iPhone and services like iTunes, music and the cloud instead of device sales or software components. The evolution of a business and being open to unlearning about the business and its function is important.

Amazon, too, is often considered an online retailer, but it long ago morphed into a platform business. Online retail capability turned into a robust media business by generating customer behaviour and spending patterns, which allowed for the creation of personalised and targeted advertising that was much more effective than that created by media companies. This required Amazon to build strong cloud storage, security and data analysis capabilities, which it then began selling as a service to other companies using the platform it built. There have been many spinoffs of what began as a warehousing and logistics business.

The kind of leader who will be successful in future will be one who constantly challenges and disrupts their own assumptions and asks hard questions.

Many businesses have watched their functions being disrupted during the pandemic, but it is an opportunity to shift focus and model. A great example of this is BottlesApp, which began as an online liquor delivery platform – a virtual bottle store. Level 5 lockdown put paid to liquor sales, which threatened the organisation's existence. The company's leaders, seeing that Pick n Pay was suddenly struggling to meet demand for online grocery deliveries, made its infrastructure available to increase Pick n Pay's capacity. The shift in business was so quick and so successful that Pick n Pay ultimately bought BottlesApp for a handsome purchase price. This is the quickness and agility that is required in adapting to changed circumstances.

The unpredictability of the future will demand opportunism. I believe that CEOs must walk the floor constantly, remain sharp and grounded, and drive opportunities hard when they present themselves. This also applies to those who aspire to lead.

On this note, successful businesses must embrace diversity of skill. In the past, most companies relied on those with accounting and financial skills, or technical product skills, to make up the talent pipeline for leadership roles. What I see now is greater value placed on the so-called softer skills. Would-be leaders who show sensitivity towards the organisation's place in society, environmental sustainability and company purpose are now being taken more seriously. The business world is evolving towards the purpose-driven organisation – businesses that are fully aware of why they exist and the difference they can make. Leaders need to know how to harness these different functions and skills, and bring them into the executive team.

In the same way, accelerating gender and racial diversity is necessary. Many companies that did not demonstrate sufficient customer insight and empathy – for example, in knowing what families were going through – were shown up during the pandemic. This is partly a result of leadership teams that were not diverse. Fortunately, I see many organisations replacing men in senior positions with powerful, highly skilled women. Vodacom has replaced its foreign, white group CFO with a local, black female CFO. MTN's new CFO is a black female. Transnet recently hired its first black female CEO, as did African Bank and Bidvest. More women are moving into executive positions and onto boards – most notably the recent appointment of female chairs at Shoprite and Capitec.

These examples are not enough, but they do reflect an international trend at multinational businesses with significant heritage, such as General Motors and Citibank.

The question is whether leaders know how to manage more diverse teams. It is not a matter of co-opting women into a male-dominated structure. Rather, leaders need to demonstrate agility and flexibility in leading diverse teams to get the best out of them in order to be successful in their careers.

In my own experience, managing a more diverse team means leading differently. I headed one of Diageo's highest-performing executive teams because I was able to get the best out of them by dealing with each person differently. The benefit for me was better business performance than if I'd had a uniformly male team, which contributed to my own success.

In a similar vein, racial integration and changing the face of leadership remains a challenge in South Africa. Again, as with males and females, there is no point in trying to clone a black leader in a white leader's image. At the same time, black leaders need to know how to deal with white colleagues who are subordinate in order to get the best out of them. They have the competencies to help you, as a leader, be successful and move the company forward. Each diverse team still needs to pull together under the same standards of performance and beliefs about company purpose.

This is even more critical at a global level. GE recently hired a chief diversity officer, which is a growing trend sparked by the Black Lives Matter movement. South Africa has not fared well in diversifying corporate leadership, enterprise development and ownership on the JSE in the last two decades. I expect there will be more pressure from the government to accelerate the process. More leaders will need to embrace and lead diversity to achieve excellent results.

We can complain about these problems and COVID-19's worsening effects, or we can roll up our sleeves and rebuild. The same agile approach must apply in dealing with governments and regulators. The reality of doing business in South Africa is that the government has an agenda to address inequality in our society. Despite problems and flaws in the approach to black economic empowerment, the unequal impact of COVID-19 on the lives of different demographic groups means that the government will certainly be trying to accelerate initiatives to reduce the unsustainable inequality that remains.

The contradictions in South Africa – of extreme wealth and poverty existing side by side, of opulent mansions and shacks – will draw more regulation, not less. Business needs to learn to embrace this agenda, rather than ignore or work against it.

There are many components of regulation which potentially increase red tape and costs for businesses in South Africa – from data privacy to encouraging development of small enterprises and fair trade to acceleration of BEE. I think that business leaders who can demonstrate superior understanding and influence the regulatory environment will advance most quickly, while avoiding becoming a victim of the hindrances of regulation.

We need reforms – especially on the labour relations side of business. As much as these reforms are needed, they can be embraced and harnessed for competitive advantage. We cannot wish governments and regulators away. Those who comply will succeed. Being seen to do the right things also becomes a competitive advantage in hiring talent.

Those who have taken short cuts, like Tongaat Hulett and Steinhoff, have suffered damaged reputations and are facing uncertain futures, with severely reduced propositions for top talent.

Government relations is far too important a factor to be passed off by a business leader. Corporate relations departments can provide access and coach the CEO. Leading from the front creates visibility that can bring economic benefits by assisting the government in delivering on its agenda.

The public and private sectors need each other – however, in South Africa they have a history of not working together effectively. Industries have cried foul – particularly during lockdown restrictions – about restricted trading and victimisation, but the government did not relent. In most cases, I assume the companies must have thought their relationship with the government was closer than it was. This is comparable with the digital antitrust and dominance accusations by various governments, which has led to claims of an onslaught on global tech businesses.

What these businesses need to acknowledge is that working within regulations produces a win–win scenario: if the businesses succeed, employ more people and make more profits, they pay more taxes and demonstrate to other companies that the country is a good investment destination where returns can be generated.

I think the point that is so often missed is that governments and business are aligned when it comes to desiring growth and profitability. Both parties need to look more closely at ways they can partner. I was encouraged by the private health sector's moves – after initially being antagonistic – to anticipate and influence government's National Health Insurance agenda by helping to set the mandate and operating model of the sector within the NHI.

The motor industry is perhaps the finest example of influencing a developmental agenda in South Africa. This sector has been able to generate a lot of profit for multinationals that have also invested billions of rands into the country. Their returns have been good, they have created many jobs and a lot of tax has been collected. There have been complaints about the automation of manufacturing facilities, but there has also been demonstrable growth in localisation of parts manufacture. This is a good example of meeting the objectives of both parties.

Many businesses are lagging from the point of view of proactively working to influence the regulator. CEOs who can contribute to the government's agenda while making money will be critical for South Africa's development. It's a skill that executives need to learn. It has worked in my favour, and good corporate citizenship is nothing to be ashamed of.

13
MY PERSONAL BOARD OF DIRECTORS

It is often said in African culture that it takes a village to raise a child. This is similar to the notion of Ubuntu: I am because we are. In this chapter, I want to celebrate the heroes and heroines who have helped me get to where I am today.

The concept is well represented in corporates through the value placed on teamwork. I was reminded of our interconnected roles in the workplace by Gary May, at the time the CEO of Guinness UDV (later Diageo South Africa) when he inducted me into the company. In one of our early meetings, he told me I should remember that we stand on the shoulders of giants. It is not for us to change or destroy the legacies of the brands we work with. We had the good fortune to be custodians of brands like Smirnoff, Johnnie Walker, Bell's and J&B – all of which were established before we were born, and will continue to exist long after we perish.

Our roles as custodians was to leave the brands in better shape than we found them in. This requires acknowledging and respecting the work of those who came before us. Just as with raising children, their success is the result of the support, opportunities, guidance and sacrifices of others.

These others I group into five categories: line managers or bosses, coaches and mentors, peers, friends and family. Line managers are the gatekeepers of your career and act somewhat like shareholders in the corporation that is you.

In my 25-year career I have had many bosses, both male and female, of various nationalities. They all approached leadership with different styles and I have tried to learn from each one. While it is no slight on any other managers I've had through the years, some have stood out more than others and I would like to celebrate their transformational contributions to my career here.

Mike Joubert was my manager at Diageo from 2000 to 2002. Though this was a relatively short time, his impact on my career and life has been enduring. What I remember particularly about Mike and what I have adapted for my own purposes is that he assembled a diverse team and managed each member differently. The importance of gaining insight into the people you manage is critical to team success.

Secondly, Mike displayed a high degree of empathy. He took a deep interest in people and encouraged their success. This was something I adopted into my own leadership style in managing others. In a word, it is empowerment. Mike would never micromanage you or breathe down your neck, but he would be clear about the outcomes required and, to attain them, he would stand by you and with you, through good and bad. Through this, he developed true trust in his team.

He was also excited about innovation and new ways of doing things. He was never satisfied with the status quo. Mike wanted us to always challenge methods and constantly move the dials, and this played directly to my personal style. I respect what exists today, but realise it may not be sufficient for me and my team to win tomorrow.

Delegation was a key component of Mike's leadership style. This was a man who was comfortable in his own skin. He wanted us to shine and was not fearful that we each had strengths that were greater than his in certain areas. He was never threatened, adopting the motto that our success was his success. The result was that we were given greater exposure early in our careers.

When I was just 23 Mike assigned me to a global Smirnoff brand relaunch project in which he was supposed to take part as the subject expert. I was the most junior on the team but he sent me to New York instead, where I ended up working with the global president of Smirnoff. This was one of the most accelerated learning phases I ever experienced. What a leader. I brought in a different voice, but it took courage and trust for him to send me in his place. Mike and I became friends over the years and today we still speak and collaborate regularly.

I still embarrass him by calling him 'boss'.

The other manager I'd like to celebrate is Herman Holtus, my second manager at P&G. Herman shaped my career in many ways because P&G was the first company I worked for. He was also a big believer in empowering his direct reports.

Herman, who hailed from the Netherlands, was very ambitious and had been tasked with a growth and development project at P&G in South Africa. He was very sharp, a fast talker and straight shooter, and was forging ahead with the establishment of a customer marketing organisation when other companies in the country hadn't even discovered the concept.

It was quite an exciting role – ensuring that the CMO was relevant and strategically important. Herman was working with some strong characters, but he wore his emotions on his sleeve and would say it like it was – there was not a lot of diplomacy about Herman, but he was quick-thinking and fast-acting, as well as amazingly articulate. This meant he could be tremendously persuasive and could sell any concept at a presentation. Once he'd obtained buy-in from the directors, he'd hand the reins to us. Herman's style was to show us how it was done and then let us get on with things. I learnt by observing him and being inspired.

Herman was also an innovator. I aspired to replicate his achievements, negotiating hard and delivering massive savings for the organisation even when it meant he had to force others into making concessions – never an easy thing to do. Despite his direct nature, Herman was a master at navigating internal corporate politics. Even when he had differences with senior executives he was still able to get the results he wanted.

He also showed me the importance of building a strong team, which has been the cornerstone of my success. Herman would leave a role vacant for a long time and suffer the consequences of a larger workload if he could not find the right talent to fill it. On this, he was relentless and uncompromising. He would rather make do with the people he had. It was exciting to watch Herman get the best out of the team members who would rise to the occasion.

The third manager who made a great impression on me was Cristina

Diezhandino, my manager at Diageo when I worked in the UK. Cristina was the marketing director for Africa, having come from a role as global brand director for Johnnie Walker. My greatest learning from Cristina was that you can be successful while being yourself. You don't have to mimic conventional methods to succeed. Success is more about outcomes. As long as you are communicating effectively about the rationale behind your methods, you're more likely to work at your best when you are being true to yourself.

Cristina's example of taking on best practice while adapting it for personal style was powerful. She had taken over from Matt Barwell, who had achieved legend status within Diageo as Africa marketing director and who was then promoted to marketing director for Europe – a huge job, and second in command in the region. These were imposing shoes to fill in a male-dominated team, but Cristina arrived and very quickly established her own unique approach.

She was comfortable and sure about what she wanted to do. Rather than simply holding the fort after Matt's departure, Cristina elected to forego any grandstanding and simply worked quietly towards delivering significant impact. Cristina never fought with anyone; her clarity of thought and ideas did the talking. She had the skill of turning down ideas with a smile in such a way that you felt you had to go back and improve on your concept to impress her.

I learnt from Cristina that humility, focus and the delivery of strong results were all that was required to become successful within a competitive multinational organisation.

Our line managers spend a lot of time with us. They are the ones who recommend us for promotion, they decide on our exposure to responsibility, review our performance and allocate workloads. They are the filter or gatekeeper to our advancement. Line managers are also responsible for mentoring and coaching us, for being sounding boards and support when we have made mistakes. Your line manager can protect you and help you bounce back. This relationship is critical to anyone's career growth. By the same token, how you play the role as a leader can be the difference between someone's success or termination of employment.

How you manage the relationship with your line manager and how they manage you is absolutely critical, though many people fail to get the best out of the relationship. This can come down to culture, gender, or other issues such as bias and favouritism; but, too few people give themselves the best chance to grow. Growth is your main agenda as an employee and you ought to take an active interest in it.

The last manager I would like to mention here is Charles Ireland, CEO of EABL. A very interesting character, Charles was very demanding yet a firm believer in servant leadership. The first time I heard of that concept was when he explained it to me: the job of a leader is to serve your direct reports and create the conditions for them to deliver and be successful.

The onus was on me to perform, but Charles was there to support me. We cannot be leaders without followers. Hence, the role is not about command and control but about a partnership to find solutions. Charles gave me complete autonomy – as far as he was concerned, there was no reason for us to discuss anything or meet if I was delivering on all my objectives. He also backed me through many tricky situations and mistakes. This made me more loyal and I worked even harder to deliver. The extent of his interaction with me was closely related to the demands of any situation – when I needed him we collaborated closely, but when he didn't need to step in he wouldn't.

A clear indication of Charles's style came when he visited Uganda during my term as CEO of UBL. He refused to address the staff because he wanted no ambiguity about who was in charge. Charles did not want to be addressed by title and went out of his way to avoid overshadowing me in my market. He had the knack of relating to people, whether over a beer or a meal or a game of golf.

He could engage you in tough, robust discussions, but he'd retain his humanity, his humility. He was never soft, but never focused on power dynamics.

All the leaders I have mentioned here were critical in shaping who I am as a leader, and the style in which I lead. They were all bold, but retained a personable edge. All of them believed in innovating, in new ideas and allowing their teams to take risks while delivering.

The next grouping in my personal board of directors is mentors. Perhaps it is because I was born to an educator, but I have maintained a massive appetite for learning throughout my life. I love feedback, critiques and appraisals in searching for ways to grow.

I believe in education that is learner-driven: when I see things I can learn or improve upon, I seek out those who are already successful in these fields and ask them to teach me. This is how I ended up with a panel of mentors I have been able to approach or watch in action through my career.

One such mentor for me was Ekwunife Okoli, one of the very few CEOs I've known who grew through the ranks of marketing and brand management. Conventional corporate wisdom is that CEOs develop in the finance stream, but Ekwunife was extremely successful as CEO of a multinational organisation with a background similar to mine and I approached him many times. He was very generous with his time, even while running a portfolio of about thirty-five countries.

Ekwunife would join me for calls and discussions to tell me how he demonstrated ability as a marketer to get corporates to trust him with balance sheet decisions. I asked him how he overcame the perceptions about marketers to be taken seriously as a businessperson. In some companies, marketing directors do not even sit on the executive committee.

I also asked him about work–life balance and conflict management, because he appeared to be universally liked. Ekwunife's experience of operating and being trusted in foreign territories – for example, working in Cameroon as a Nigerian – was invaluable to me since South Africa has not enjoyed a great reputation on the continent thanks to xenophobic violence against African nationals back home. Part of my role while based in Uganda was winning hearts and minds as a South African executive.

Ekwunife would end up playing an important role in my career in terms of building my confidence and dealing with my insecurities. It was inspiring to have a role model for getting to the top along my path. Our backgrounds and approaches were similar and he turned into a challenging, supportive and close friend who pushed me hard.

I was also conscious that Ekwunife did all of this because he appeared to enjoy it – he had no ulterior motive for doing so. From time to time I still call upon him.

Another of my mentors was Charles Mead, the professional CEO coach at YFC – a talent development and leadership consultancy in the UK. I benefitted from the wealth of knowledge Charles was able to impart, but what I really valued was his trained approach. He practised the Socratic method to perfection, never giving me answers but facilitating conversations to uncover solutions. He was a master at forcing me to be creative in finding solutions. I would never leave a conversation with Charles feeling as though I had final, definitive answers. It was always an intriguing process where I looked forward to our next engagement. I was constantly challenged and aware that I was undergoing personal growth.

My engagements with Charles gave me confidence rooted in reflection. As executives, we can become so busy that we do not take time to stop and think. Charles taught me to regularly confront my thoughts and assumptions so that I was never operating on autopilot. This was a process of benchmarking – peeling back the onion, and always asking why.

Gerald Mahinda, MD of Sub-Saharan Africa at the Kellogg Company, played an important role in demonstrating that a leader could make a great impact even as a relatively introverted individual. Gerald was inquisitive and curious, a lover of innovation and a highly supportive mentor. He told me about his disappointment at having to leave Diageo without fulfilling his ambition to become a global executive director and president for Africa. When it became clear that he was not considered a frontrunner for the position, he decided it was time to search for his next role externally, ultimately joining Kellogg.

Gerald's description of his personal disappointment helped me build resilience. If CEOs I admired could suffer enormous setbacks, failures and fallouts, I needed to be pragmatic about my measurement of success and appreciate that none of us will ever enjoy uninterrupted progress to the top.

We will be victims of politics. We will fall, and fall hard. This is where friends and family step in, if you're lucky enough to have them.

I consider myself fortunate to have been able to call on Gerald for lessons from his experience. This meant I would never walk into similar situations blindly.

Many others have shaped my approach as a life coach and mentor. Among them are superiors, peers, lecturers and coaches who have all generously given their time and experience to allow me to benefit from their learnings. When I have identified something I could learn from, I have been unafraid to approach people and ask – always overwhelmed by people's generosity in their guidance and support when I do so. Not enough of us raise our hands to ask for help. It has worked for me and my career.

The third grouping within my personal board of directors is my fellow directors and board peers. I have had the pleasure of sitting on four boards as an independent non-executive director, ranging from listed property to financial services providers to manufacturers and distributors of soft drinks and distributors of electronics accessories.

This diversity speaks of my attitude to business: I believe it helps to have a depth of industry experience but I learn fastest by engaging with different industries and looking for commonalities. These provide the inspiration for adapting and renovating ideas. In this way, it is possible to make moves your competitors could not foresee.

I have found more commonalities than differences, which has allowed me to contribute value. More importantly, I get to learn from astute executives and entrepreneurs who have built amazing businesses. While my involvement with these boards could be construed as the top rung of business, my learning has never stopped. In fact, I have learnt more, and faster, in the two years of sitting on these boards than ever before.

Here, I found experienced business leaders who look to their boards for guidance and strategic challenges. They are achievers in their own right and we get to witness them in action, which is very useful as a CEO – it enables me to compare and contrast decisions and actions with my own.

When I consider the level of involvement of someone like Jeffrey Wapnick, MD of listed property company Octodec, I see someone who takes an intense interest in his customers, walking the streets, visiting buildings, noting cracked windows and dirty floors, chasing up non-payment. He knows his business back to front in a way most of us can only aspire to. This intimate knowledge of your business is where opportunities lie.

Similarly, the co-founders of mobile device and accessories distributor Gammatek – Gary Tooch and Warren Berman – have been running the business for 20 years and they are only in their forties. This is a massive business, with leading market share in South Africa, which sold to private equity player Ethos for R1 billion. The chemistry between them, their energy and their passion, is inspiring for someone like me, who has a low boredom threshold. I love the enjoyment factor at play in their business – they look like they love what they're doing and happen to make good money from it. How do I instil that in myself and my employees?

Entrepreneurs operate with a risk appetite and speed of decision making and execution which should be the envy of any corporate. How can I bring this flair into a business? How do I cut down on red tape to run a big business as though it was small without compromising governance? These are valuable lessons to learn.

The central learning from entrepreneurs is that businesses should be lean. If you look at how and where they spend money, you'll understand what it means to be a lean enterprise. I see fat everywhere I look at corporates. Gammatek's turnover and margins are large, but the company employs just 100 people. By contrast, many corporate leaders take pride in quoting a large staff complement. For me, if a job can be done with fewer people, it should be. This is what drives profitability and sustainability. Leaders should never benchmark by staff complement to feel successful – this is for government to do. In business, being lean and making profit means being able to invest elsewhere, buy other companies and ultimately employ more people that way. Efficiency is the key.

Learning was the main reason I joined boards. I needed experience and skill in balance sheet management and governance of an entire organisation. As someone aspiring to be the CEO of a listed entity, I had witnessed several governance breaches that hit the headlines, such as at Steinhoff, African Bank, VBS, Tongaat Hulett and McKinsey. I asked myself how these failures could have occurred under the watch of each board, and how I could play a role in ensuring that CEOs worked more honestly and that governance was enshrined in business operations.

Transparency and honesty ensure long-term wealth creation for shareholders and an avoidance of governance failures. I wanted to find ways to ensure that boards and executives could work together more effectively, and the only way to learn about it was to immerse myself in it – sink or swim. I'm not the type of person who sinks.

My growth through sitting on these boards has been a result of the diversity of skills my fellow board members have brought to the table. Many boards still need to transform both demographically and in terms of skills. Most boards are stacked with former accountants, CEOs or CFOs. Homogeneity does not produce effective boards. To me, public relations and corporate communications, accounting, auditing and human resources backgrounds are important to bring together – especially from a social and ethics committee point of view.

These so-called softer skills allow for the creation of a truly purpose-led organisation. People who are commercially astute when it comes to sales, marketing and strategy can ask the right questions about the operations of the organisation. If you don't have those diverse skills to identify strategic gaps – which management may either fail to see or even hide deliberately – you cannot ensure effective governance.

Boards are demanding of one's time. This is why many board members are experienced executives who have retired or are over the age of 55 and working part-time. In many cases I have been the youngest board member. This has enabled me to learn from the wealth of experience of my fellow board members. Just being in board meetings or strategy sessions is an incredible opportunity to learn by observation.

Of course, I still need to bring my own voice to the table – I could not sit on these boards without contributing value – but I often marvel at the ways my peers of advanced ages remain sharp and see things others could not. I choose to bask in the experience they bring and the humility with which they contribute. I have often asked questions privately over coffee because my fellow board members have so much knowledge to impart.

Participating on these boards has allowed me to benchmark externally, which I've found invaluable in preparing for my future. However, education can also provide similar learnings. Completing my MBA through the University of Cape Town, I learnt much from case studies, literature and lecturers. Exposure to corporate training, such as executive training programmes, is a valid way of benchmarking externally.

This grouping within my personal board of directors includes my non-competing peers – my network of executives who are doing similar jobs in similar situations in different industries, countries and companies. I have found leveraging this network for support to be incredibly useful.

Many executives belong to organisations and networks of like-minded individuals outside of their companies, such as Rotary organisations. I have mentioned that I was recruited to the Young Presidents' Organization about three years ago, joining CEOs under 45 from various sizes and types of organisations. You pay a subscription to belong to a chapter of YPO and are then placed in a forum with five to seven other, non-competing CEOs with whom you can talk about anything: share frustrations, opportunities, issues and learnings by being in the conversation. This has been an invaluable support mechanism for me.

Beyond this, YPO has provided many resources, such as portals, literature and courses to attend. It really is a holistic approach to leadership support, even including a family component. I found that, though the tasks we face daily as business leaders may be daunting, they are not unique. We share our problems and learn to deal with them together.

YPO is a global organisation, so its context and lessons are not bound by geography, culture or environment. I learn about new situations simply by requesting meetings, which has given me new perspectives on my business challenges. I have also assumed a leadership role within the Pretoria chapter of YPO, becoming chief financial officer. This has allowed me to interact more with the chapter and the people affiliated with it.

Highlights of these interactions include being invited to facilitate a conversation with the legendary entrepreneur Wendy Luhabe. This was an exclusive and intimate session limited to about ten participants, where she shared her wisdom and real-life lessons with us. The pleasure of planning for the event, conducting the interview and learning from her responses was immense – we delved into boardroom politics, driving a presence as a 'boardroom minority' and creating impact.

I was also facilitator for a session featuring Gareth Ackerman, chair of Pick n Pay. It was fascinating to listen to his account of his career, coming to terms with living in the shadow of his parents and ultimately giving up executive control of the company when he realised someone else could do a better job. There was much to learn about leadership in his story.

More recently, YPO invited the CEO of Remgro, Jannie Durand, who was previously chief of staff for Anton Rupert. Jannie was in his forties when he assumed this role, controlling a strong portfolio of businesses in which the Rupert family is invested. Being responsible for delivering the expected returns would cause many would-be CEOs to wilt.

YPO has also brought together young business leaders and keynote speakers as diverse as Silicon Valley entrepreneurs and presidents of African countries. We have learnt much and engaged deeply to uncover opportunities together.

When I moved to General Electric I joined the oil and gas workstreams of YPO, which provided me with so many resources and new contacts to learn from. Almost instantly, other leaders were accessible to me.

Alumni associations and other peer organisations can fulfil similar roles for executives, allowing for ongoing learning and growth in a safe environment with like-minded individuals. Many CEOs even cultivate informal groupings of friends which can provide enhancement, learning and growth. I belong to such a group, called Malipathi Investments, which was set up to take advantage of B-BBEE opportunities. Collectively, we – as a group of professionals from various backgrounds – invest and are paid dividends over the years. We learn a lot from each other when we meet for annual general meetings.

About thirty of us started a cattle investment group, which means I have also learnt about managing livestock. We also have a group called the Whisky Social Club, which meets every other month with a rotating roster of hosts. The host is presented with a special bottle of rare whisky while they, in turn, provide entertainment, intellectual stimulation, debate topics and refreshments.

These events have brought in guest speakers ranging from a speaker of Parliament to the founder of a digital transformation firm, the CEO of a union investment arm and a top artist who exhibits internationally.

When you mingle with such diverse crowds you are bound to learn something new. How can Nelson Makamo's story of building his business as an artist help me as a business leader? This is external benchmarking and co-opetition – competing while co-operating, sharing experiences and comparing notes.

By stark contrast with my peers and fellow board members, the next category within my personal board of directors – my friends – are people who shape and mould me as a person, despite not necessarily occupying similar roles in the business world. It may surprise people to learn that friends can have such an impact on our professional lives, but I would have floundered without the encouragement, support and honest critique of my true friends – most of whom have known me for at least the two decades since I was at school or university.

I don't have many friends at this level and we have watched each other grow, fail and succeed in equal measure as individuals, parents and professionals. When I'm not sure about something I feel safe talking with them and they, in turn, want nothing more than for me to be happy. Collectively, we call ourselves the Big Five: Thabo Mogobe, Refilwe Tshabalala, Vuyani Mdaka, Sammy Mafu and me.

Our relationships are not without their ups and downs, but the thing about true friends is that they provide the space for you to be you, without fear of being judged. Drink what you want to drink, dance the way you want to (and they'll tell you I have two left feet), feel unburdened of the sometimes-oppressive weight of leadership responsibility. When it comes to questions about important milestones and career moves, we compare notes in a safe and supportive environment.

As executives it can be difficult to discern the motives of people who approach us – it is often for personal gain: the next project, a promotion, a tender, or other motives. There is a lot of fakery around us and the pressure to always give the best account of ourselves can be tiring. Good friends are not simply praise singers.

Most importantly, friends put us in our place – often with completely innocent commentary. Many of my friends are not in the same industries or business lines, but they can offer perspectives that come from good intentions. I rely on my friends to tell me when I am deviating from what we collectively consider to be our values, as well as to help me bounce back from personal tragedy. They can step in to help me when I feel overwhelmed.

The diversity of backgrounds within my circle of friends – across politics, doing business with government and law, for example – allows me to draw on their experience in a manner similar to my board peers. I learn from the ways my friends lead themselves, as the CEOs of themselves, so that I may practise the same.

I have learnt much in terms of recovering from personal and professional setbacks, juggling work–life balance and navigating multiple board commitments from my friends.

Friendships have brought new possibilities, too. Dr Howard Manyonga and I founded an investment club, which drew us closer together. As a gynaecologist, Howard has involved himself in business and investment activities far beyond what you would expect, which I found encouraging in its similarity to my preferred method of learning and growing. Our role models can come from any background.

My personal board of directors would not be complete without my family. I have been blessed with a wonderful, loving and progressive wife, Mosima. It is a cliché and sounds sexist to repeat the adage that behind every successful man there stands a woman but, allowing that the reverse is true, it is virtually impossible to achieve any level of success without a supportive partner.

Having someone to support you in your success can take many forms.

I was told by my coaches that it is lonely at the top and I have found this to be true. At a certain point people are reluctant to talk to you because they either cannot relate to your position or are intimidated. Attaining the upper reaches of any career can cause you to drift apart from others. For this reason, it is common to hear of executives speak of intimate conversations with their partners – so-called pillow talk. Even when president, Barack Obama claimed that Michelle was actually running the country. This is to recognise the important roles our spouses, partners or supporters play in our success. In my case, there are many ways in which Mosima has supported me.

I cannot underestimate how difficult this must have been for her, given that she was a professional in her own right. The spouses of executives frequently opt to give up their jobs to take on the responsibility of running the household in order to free up the executives' time, but Mosima is a serious professional and a healthcare executive who has also needed me to support her in her own career growth.

This has been an incredibly rewarding exchange, illustrated by a few highlights from our time together. When I took the decision to start my own business with Nando's in 2006, we were newlyweds. I decided to cash in my pension to invest in the business, which not only took away my pension but my full-time job and salary.

Mosima was not earning much at the time, in her first year of practising medicine doing her internship. She had another year of community service to face in 2007 before she could establish a private practice. Nevertheless, she was behind me all the way, making sure we did what it took to make the business work. In the years since I have ventured into various business opportunities, sometimes making money, sometimes losing it, she's supported these moves, though not without critique. She forces me to rethink when my capacity is stretched.

That ability to be challenged and questioned is valuable. It also confirmed my belief that experience is overrated. Business decisions are about consumers, and we are all consumers. The profit calculation is actually very simple.

A few years later I decided to give up the Nando's business and – while we were expecting our first child – asked her to put her flourishing career on hold for us to move to the UK. We thought long and hard about the decision, which would inevitably slow her professional progress, but I promised I'd find a way to repay her for backing me.

It was a big leap. To her credit, Mosima used the opportunity to enrol for her MBA at Oxford and convert her career from the clinical side of medicine to the management and consulting arena. She started a successful management consulting career with McKinsey and then Accenture. This silver lining took months of frustrating sacrifice and a period in which she was unable to work.

My wife inspires me. Like me, she is competitive. What she has achieved at her age – despite my ten-year head start in working – is impressive. She told me I had the advantage of time, but promised me her income would one day overtake mine. We enjoy a positive, healthy competition that keeps us both pushing for progress. I know few people who work as hard as she does, waking up at 3 a.m. to exercise, work, prepare meals and get the kids to school – her capacity is incredible.

Even when I am pushing hard at my own work I see her level of energy, passion and dedication and know that I cannot let up. She brings her work ethic to her fitness and her private work, too. Mosima taught me that you do what you can with what you have. When she started her MBA at Oxford we did not get the scholarship we hoped for and had to take on some debt to cover the fees. She took on a part-time job working nights at a hospital. I could not believe she found time to complete her assignments and attend classes, but even in South Africa as a community doctor she would live on two to three hours of sleep a night to work extra shifts to bring home more pay.

I learnt that it's all about choices: if something is important to you, you'll make time for it. I am less daunted about the time available to me in a day, as a result. Billionaires have 24 hours in a day like the rest of us; they just use the time more smartly.

Though Mosima had worked so hard to establish her consulting career, when I was given the opportunity to take up the role of CEO at UBL she was again confronted with a difficult scenario. McKinsey did not have a presence in Uganda, which meant she would have to give up exciting projects and a lucrative career to come with me. I initially proposed commuting, but she said no – partly on account of expecting our second child at the time.

I admire her spiritual take on life's turns – that she acknowledges that we cannot always be in control. Mosima has rolled with life's punches – here she was, a trained medical professional, working as a management consultant for every kind of client from financial institutions to power stations. She has demonstrated an ability to leverage a sharp mind and core principles in novel and surprising ways, which dovetails with my experience in business.

As a direct result, I did a stint in consulting with the Boston Consulting Group. I am glad I did, learning a great deal about many different businesses and industries in just 18 months. The outcome was that I became a board member of a financial services firm.

There is a lot we learn from our partners. My children, likewise, can provide nudges of inspiration. I find parenting challenging, particularly when we are forced to confront and deal with behaviour that deviates from our expectations. It has forced me to be honest about the time I was investing in parenting and find ways to support and inspire my children. How can I inspire my employees if I cannot get the best out of my kids?

Ultimately, we want to provide our children with the best platform for their own success, which can inspire us to work harder and leverage our networks to showcase to them the opportunities that lie in wait.

Simple, innocent conversations can bring great enlightenment. Children tell it like it is. My youngest has the habit of complaining about the work I do and its impact on the time I spend with him. We cannot forget our humanity – at home I am not a CEO but a father, a husband. My family demands quality time and a deeper entrenchment in these bonds can give me the joy and hope I need to pursue my core purpose.